# A Blessed Journey

### Through Terminal Cancer Into Divine Healing

*by*
Cindy Cox

*A Blessed Journey*
ISBN 0-88144-237-2
Copyright © 2006 by
Cindy Cox
Christian Illness Support
14418 Knightsbridge Dr.
Shelby Twp., MI 48315
www.ablessedjourney.com

Published by
Victory Graphics & Media
9731 E. 54th Street
Tulsa, OK 74146.

Text Design: Bobby and Lisa Simpson
               www.simpsonproductions.net
Cover Design: Keigh Cox

# Dedication

**To Kent,**
**my husband, my best friend, the love of my life.**
This new season of our life has been so incredible.
Do you know what I love the most? I love our conversations
which so frequently center around the works of our amazing
heavenly Father, sometimes burning with a holy zeal that
comes through the anointing of our healing ministry,
sometimes gentle and quiet and saturated with the peace of our
Lord, but always, always filled with unconditional love and
support for one another. I am the most blessed
woman in the world to have you for my husband!
And I love you the most!


**To Jennifer,**
**my dear friend who introduced me to Jesus.**
Without you, and without Him, these words would never
have been written. Thank you, Jenn, for saying "yes" to the
leading of the Holy Spirit, and for being bold enough to share
the truth with me. Thank you for always being there to answer
my many questions, to pray with me, to mentor me.
I am very alive … physically, spiritually, and eternally …
because of you!
You are my hero!

To Mianne,
my sister, and my spiritual friend.
I am still amazed at the discovery that I have an on-fire-for-
God, Spirit-filled sister! You were one of the few people who
had absolute faith that our Mighty God is bigger than the
cancer that the doctors said was incurable. You never wavered.
You never doubted. Your immense faith and your fervency in
sharing that faith led others to stand strong right beside you! I
love you, my sister, and I thank you for waiting with open
arms for me to return to you!
I assure you, I'm here to stay!


**And, to God Almighty,**
**The Author of my life!**
There aren't words in this language to give to You the
thanksgiving and praise and adoration that my heart pours out
for You. I am in awe of Your loving-kindness and Your tender
mercies! To think that You had me in mind when You sent
Your beloved Son, Jesus, to pay the price for my redemption
and for my reservation in Heaven with You!
You gave me life, and now I choose to live my life for You!
Here am I, Lord.
Send me!

# *Acknowledgments*

Thank you to my spiritual mama, Pastor Marie Bernier, Senior Pastor of Life Christian Church in Troy, Michigan. You have such a heart of love for God and for His people. Hebrews 13:7 NIV says, *Remember your leaders, who spoke the word of God to you. Consider the outcome of their way of life and imitate their faith.* As I consider the outcome of your way of life, I see so clearly the mature fruit of the Spirit! You are truly connected to the Vine! I strive to imitate your life of faith, Pastor Marie, living to love and serve God and His people. Thank you for bringing the Word of God into my life with clarity, teaching me how to apply the Word and how to live an overcoming life.

Thank you to the Life Bible Institute, a two-year Bible school offered through Life Christian Church. Pastor Tracy Boyd, Pastor Dino Lasala, and Pastor Anton Lasala are amazing, anointed teachers of the Word. The foundation of my faith is not built upon sand, but upon rock. The content of this book is based upon the faith foundation that was engrafted into my spirit through the process of the Life Bible Institute.

Thank you to Minister Jane Zwicker, my own personal editor and friend … who has provided me with greatly appreciated feedback, in order to ensure that this book is scripturally accurate and securely founded upon the Word of God.

And thank you, Father God, for calling me to write this book. You don't call the qualified, You qualify the called. It is only through You, through the healing blood of Jesus, and through the anointing of Your Holy Spirit, that *A Blessed Journey* has become a reality.

# Contents

# Part One

# HEALED OF CANCER

*Bless the Lord, O my soul, and forget not all His benefits: Who forgives all your iniquities, Who heals all your diseases, Who redeems your life from destruction, Who crowns you with lovingkindness and tender mercies, Who satisfies your mouth with good things so that your youth is renewed like the eagle's.*
Psalm 103:2-5

God has done a mighty work in my life.
I bless the Lord with all that is deep within me!
I bless His holy name!

*P*art One of *A Blessed Journey* gives an account of the faith journey that I have begun. It is my testimony of healing of Stage 4 incurable melanoma and God's treatment plan. Unlike so many cancer books you may pick up, this one has hope and faith as its central themes. It brings not only good news, but the best news! And that news is for you as well as for me!

Shortly after my own healing, my husband and I began ministering individually to the sick, and have been honored to witness God's healing in so very many broken bodies. One year after receiving divine healing of cancer, God laid it heavy on my heart to share my story beyond the limits of the spoken word. So I started to write. This is the story that God gave to me to give to you.

*Chapter One*

# THE FIRST STEP

*I shall not die, but live, and declare the works of the Lord.*
Psalm 118:17

So begins my declaration.

February 19, 2002, was the first day of my new life.

*I* am one of those "Type-A" personalities who strive to do everything to perfection. Every day of my life prior to February 19, 2002, I would set my alarm for 4:45 a.m., I would hit the snooze button once and only once, and dragging myself out of bed I would exercise for a half hour before showering. Each day I had a detailed list of things to complete. Only when I had kept all my scheduled appointments and completed all my listed tasks did I achieve what I believed to be another successful and fulfilling day.

On February 19, 2002, I had my alarm set at 4:45 a.m. And I probably did hit the snooze button once and only once. But when I got up that day, for the very first time in my life, I devoted time to God. That morning in February, the dreariest month of the year, proved to be the first glimpse of light on my journey.

God's grace is so amazing! On this February morning, the Holy Spirit was drawing me close, opening the eyes of my heart to be enlightened to the truth of God's Word! I had a list of scriptures that a friend had suggested for me to read. I had never been a Bible reader. I had tried occasionally, but it just didn't speak to me. However, these particular scriptures truly DID speak to me. I had a desperate need in my life, and I was searching for an answer. Since these scriptures were so meaningful to me, I decided to type them into my computer so I could refer to them frequently and easily. After I had finished typing them into the computer, I clicked "Save." In Microsoft Word, when you save a document, the first line you have typed appears in the "File Name" box. But that is not what happened on February 19, 2002. The file name that automatically appeared in the file name box was: *Messages from God.*

Was God really speaking to me? At that time, I didn't realize that God's Word is living and always speaks to believers! I had no idea just how powerful God and His Word are. Then, just as I was sitting there in awe contemplating how in the world that title had appeared on my document, the electricity went off! The computer screen faded to black nothingness. The lights were extinguished. The room was in absolute darkness. The awesome presence of God was with me, and I was utterly terrified.

I believe that God was speaking to me that morning ... loud and clear. There was no explanation for the electricity to go off. There was no storm, no wind. Rather, the power of my mighty God was at work!

The electricity came back on within a brief moment. I got ready and went to work, but God's message and its implications had sparked something within me, which would rapidly begin a raging spiritual fire.

God sent me an angel. Her name is Jenny. She is a teacher and she worked in the same school where I am a Learning Consultant. Jenny is a devout Christian who lives her life for God. She is the friend who had suggested the scriptures that I read that morning.

As soon as I got to school that day, I went to tell her about my *Messages from God* and the electricity failure. She immediately began talking to me about sickness and healing truths from God's Word that I had never heard before. I later realized that the anointing of the Holy Spirit was flowing through her. God was speaking to me through Jenny.

To tell you the truth, I don't even really remember what we talked about during those few precious minutes. But I do know that Jenny asked me if I was saved, to which I replied, "I'm not sure. I think I am. I live a good life. I go to church every Sunday. I've received all of the sacraments." Jenny replied with a simple question, "Do you want to be sure?"

Right then and there, in Jenny's cramped workroom, we prayed together the prayer of salvation. As troops of first graders filed into the room with their show-and-tell, school bags, and notes for their teacher, I accepted Jesus as my Lord and Savior with tears of grace flowing down my cheeks.

February 19, 2002, was the first day of my new life.

---

But I need to back up before I go ahead.

## Chapter Two

# THE DEPTHS OF DESPAIR

*L*et me go back and start at the beginning.

My dear friend Jenny gave those healing scriptures to me because I had just been diagnosed with terminal cancer. I was broken, sick, and deep in the depths of despair. Fear was consuming my soul more completely than the cancer that was consuming my flesh.

If you are reading this book right now because you have been diagnosed with cancer, please, please, please continue to read. When I was diagnosed with cancer, I could not read anything to do with information about cancer or treatments. It tore me up inside. My guts were wrenched; the fear within me welled up so desperately that I felt life was being extinguished within me with each word I read.

But this book is not about the science of cancer or about medical treatments. It is about God's healing, which is available to everyone!

My mission in writing this book is to help cancer patients and their loved ones to move beyond the depths of despair and into the realm of peace. My purpose is to reveal the way to overcome the fear, the way to grow spiritually and physically into a new person, better than the pre-cancer person that you once were, whole and healthy in body, soul, and spirit. My intention is to bring healing to the sick, and to give God all of the glory!

This is the only chapter of my book that is dismal. I will keep it short and simple because my story is not dismal. It is joyous!

## My First Forty-Three Years of Life

I loved summer and heat, and sun, sun, sun! I spent every weekend at the cottage on the deck and in the water, and went on two warm weather vacations every winter – each preceded by a month of tanning booths! No sunscreen over SPF 8 ever touched my skin. However, since I spent so much time in the sun, I made sure to have a skin exam every year or two.

## January 8, 2002

After a routine skin check, my dermatologist removed a suspicious mole from my buttock, of all places! (No more tanning booths for me!)

## January 18, 2002

I received a call from my dermatologist confirming a positive biopsy. I had melanoma. I was referred to the University of Michigan Medical Center for a consultation.

## JANUARY 23, 2002

At my first appointment, I was quickly assured that the depth of the original mole was shallow, and that it would be very unlikely that the melanoma had spread any further (Stage 1). However, after a brief exam, the doctor noticed a swollen lymph node in my right groin and ordered a fine needle biopsy of the node that same day.

## JANUARY 25, 2002

I received a phone call from the doctor I had consulted with earlier in the week. The pathology report from the fine needle biopsy was positive for melanoma in the lymph node, which moved me directly into Stage 3. (Melanoma is considered Stage 2 if the mole is larger or deeper, but has not moved into the lymph node system.)

The doctor informed me that I would require a lymph node dissection (removal of a whole mass of tissue) followed by a year of Interferon treatment. Interferon is similar to a substance made by the body's immune system. This drug fights cancer cells and stimulates the body's immune system to work better … but it also has some very negative side effects such as fatigue, depression, nausea, and diarrhea. Although the diagnosis was bleak, the cancer was still considered curable.

## FEBRUARY 8, 2002

I had my pre-op appointment with the surgeon who would perform the lymph node dissection, which was scheduled for February 20. That same afternoon, I had a routine CT scan to rule out further metastasis, or spreading, of the melanoma.

## FEBRUARY 13, 2002

I received another call from the University of Michigan Medical Center. The CT scan indicated the spread of melanoma throughout my lymphatic system; in my groin, in my lower abdomen, in the vicinity of my diaphragm, and in my neck. The metastasis of melanoma into the lymphatic chain is considered Stage 4 and incurable. He cancelled the scheduled surgery, clearly stating that it would do no good if the cancer had spread to other lymph nodes.

I received that phone call at the end of the workday. I went home in shock and put something together for dinner. I clearly remember sitting down at the dinner table that night with my husband and daughter. I had absolutely no appetite, and though I tried to be strong, I broke down into racking sobs as I plunged into the deepest depths of despair, of indescribable gut-wrenching, consuming terror.

I was scheduled to leave for Alabama the following day for a long weekend with my parents. I decided to go ahead with the trip, but it was probably the most difficult, soul-wrenching experience I've ever had. My parents wanted so much to console me, to help me, to take away the cancer. But that simply wasn't possible. I put on a forced smile, and made attempts at small talk, but inside I was overflowing with fear and hopelessness.

I remember walking the Gulf Shore beach, talking to a distant God whom I barely knew. I kept questioning His will. Was it the will of God for me to have cancer? Was it the will of God for me to die and to leave my children and my husband? Was it the will of God for me to never see my children's children? I prayed with utter desperation to God. I tried so hard to be strong, but I was so scared, so alone.

Most of us have prayed a prayer like this at one point or another in our lifetimes. Before you read one more page of this book, let me assure you, the answer is **NO**, it is **NOT** our heavenly Father's will for His children to be sick, to suffer pain and disease. Would it ever be your will for your natural children to be sick or to die of cancer? Of course not! And God loves you with a compassion that overshadows any love we have ever known.

I returned home from Alabama on Monday, February 18. The next day, the 19th, was the day God gave me His message, the day that I received Jesus as my Lord and Savior. The dismal, fear-filled expectation of a miserable death was behind me, and my new life and healing had begun! Praise my God!!!

## Chapter Three

# THE JOURNEY BEGINS

On February 19, 2002, my friend Jenny also brought me my first *rhema* word from the Bible. A *rhema* word is a word of revelation, an individual scripture which the Holy Spirit brings to us in a time of need. The Word was from the third epistle of John, verse 2. It says, *Beloved, I pray that you may prosper in all things and be in health, just as your soul prospers.* I claimed that Word with my whole heart! I am God's beloved! He desires that I prosper in all things and that I'm in health in body, mind, and spirit! I have held onto this precious scripture with my entire being! It has been so wonderfully manifested, and continues to increase as I grow in my relationship with my Lord!

As I look back now, I realize that I was totally open to receive this promise from God. I had been handed a death sentence. I had no medical hope. All I had was the hope of a miracle from God. Hope is important, but it lacks substance until filled with faith.

As my journey began, Jenny shared three fundamental truths with me. These seeds that were planted took root in the fertile soil God had prepared within my heart, and rapidly grew deep, sturdy roots of a mighty, powerful faith.

### FUNDAMENTAL TRUTH #1: IT IS ALWAYS GOD'S WILL TO HEAL!

When Jesus was alive on this earth, He healed ALL who came to Him. He never denied healing to anyone. And *Jesus Christ is the same yesterday, today, and forever!* (Hebrews 13:8). Therefore it follows that it is the will of God to heal all today just as it was when Jesus was walking on this earth in the form of a man!

Then the immediate question is, why are so many people sick and dying? At first, I didn't even go there. I came to God as a child, with childlike faith. I simply believed, trusted, and obeyed Him, as a young child believes, trusts, and obeys his earthly parents. (In chapter 20 I will elaborate on the fundamental truth that it is ALWAYS God's perfect will to heal.)

What did I do with this information? I began to devour scriptures regarding the miraculous healings in Jesus' day. There are twenty-three healing miracles performed by Jesus and written about in the four Gospels. I read and studied all of the accounts of these miracles over and over and over again.

### FUNDAMENTAL TRUTH #2: JESUS DIED FOR OUR HEALING!

Christians agree that Jesus died for the forgiveness of our sins. But there's more. The sin in our lives opens the door to sickness and disease. With the forgiveness of sins, provided through the death and resurrection of Jesus, the door to sickness and disease is slammed shut! Hallelujah!

But don't take my word for it; take God's Word. The Bible confirms this truth. Isaiah 53:4-5 says: *Surely He has borne our griefs and carried our sorrows ... He was wounded for our transgressions, He was bruised for our iniquities; the chastisement for our peace was upon Him, and by His stripes we are healed.*

Now I want to share some clarifications of the underlined words in this scripture. The word "griefs" in the original Hebrew means sickness or disease. "Sorrows" means pain. "Transgressions" and "iniquities" are intentional and unintentional sin. The word "chastisement" means penalty or price, and the word "peace" in the original Hebrew is *shalom,* which means safety, prosperity, and health.

If I were to substitute these more familiar words for the biblical words, this scripture would read: Surely He (Jesus) has borne our sickness and disease and carried our pain ... He was wounded for our intentional and unintentional sins. The penalty for our safety, our prosperity, and our health was upon Him; and by His stripes we are healed and made whole!

When Jenny shared this truth with me, I had never heard it before, and I didn't fully understand, but again, I accepted it through childlike faith. One awesome thing I've come to realize is that God always meets us right where we are, and then holds our hand as He lovingly leads and guides us until we gradually become ready to receive more. (Chapter 19 will elaborate on "The Great Exchange," the fundamental truth that Jesus died for our healing.)

## Fundamental Truth #3: There is power in the Word.

Proverbs 4:20-22 NIV says, *My son, pay attention to what I say; listen closely to my words. Do not let them out of your sight, keep them within your heart; for they are life to those who find them and health to a man's whole body.* This scripture says that the Word of God is life and health, IF we pay attention, listen closely, do not let them out of our sight, and keep them within our heart!

Another wonderful scripture in Romans 10:17 says, *So then faith comes by hearing, and hearing by the word of God.* This scripture reveals that hearing God's Word builds faith. And faith is necessary for receiving healing. Jesus required faith and purity of heart when He healed the sick in His days on earth. What then is this faith? Hebrews 11:1 says, *Now faith is the substance of things hoped for, the evidence of things not seen.* Faith is not believing just what we see. Faith is completely believing God's Word above what we see; i.e., believing God's report that *by His stripes we were healed* over the medical diagnosis of cancer! Verse 6 goes on to say, *But without faith it is impossible to please Him, for he who comes to God must believe that He is, and that He is a rewarder of those who diligently seek Him.* This scripture tells us that in order to receive our reward, we must have faith and diligently seek God!

Jenny gave me a tiny but powerful book titled *The Creative Power for Healing* by Charles Capps. In this little booklet, Charles Capps has collected many scriptures related to healing. Many are paraphrased to directly relate to specific types of sicknesses; in my case, cancer. I immediately began declaring these healing scriptures over myself three times a day. I personalized them even more to meet my explicit needs and prayed them fervently! They were (and still are) my daily medicine. And gradually, with the power of God's Word, my faith began to grow stronger and stronger until I knew that I knew that I knew that God had healed my body completely and perfectly. The initial seed of hope grew into a solid faith that professed, "Yes, my Jesus healed cancer when He died for me. I receive that healing in the name of Jesus!"

This was my starting point. I received the seed that it IS God's will to heal. I learned and believed with all my heart that Jesus died not only for forgiveness of sins, but also for all that accompanies sin, including sickness. And I immediately began declaring the healing scriptures over the disease in my body.

My blessed journey had begun!

## Chapter Four

# HEALING HANDS

On February 22, I attended Jenny's church for the first time. It is a nondenominational, full gospel, Holy Spirit-filled church. She had invited me because a faith healer was going to be visiting and preaching, and I would have the opportunity for him to lay hands on me and pray over me for healing. There are several scriptural ways that God heals. They include:

- ✞ Laying on of hands (Mark 16:17-18).
- ✞ Prayer of agreement (Matthew 18:18-20).
- ✞ Prayer cloth (Acts 19:11-12).
- ✞ The healing gift of the Spirit (1 Corinthians 12:9).
- ✞ Call for the elders (James 5:14).
- ✞ Your own faith (Mark 11:23-24).

I would suggest that you take time to read the Bible scriptures to see for yourself that God heals in many ways. I believe my healing was a result of several of these, including the laying on of hands, the prayer of agreement, and my own faith.

My husband, my brother and his wife went with me to this prayer meeting as a support. Jenny had ministered to me throughout the week by providing healing scriptures, instructing me to read, reread, and meditate on them, and encouraging me to go to the meeting <u>expecting</u> to receive healing, just like the people in the scriptures received from Jesus!

The service began with praise and worship, which I had never experienced before. I had always loved music, but I had never gone further than simply singing songs in church. I had never freely poured out my love and praise to God through song. During the service, the music went on and on and on, with choruses repeated over and over again. Between songs, people openly expressed their praise and worship to God with total abandonment. I didn't understand this free worship.

As I witnessed the church praising and worshipping, I struggled to stand upright, holding onto the pew in front of me for support because I was in intense pain. From the day I had received the Stage 4 cancer diagnosis, symptoms had started to appear in my body. I could actually feel the enlarged lymph nodes in my groin, abdomen, and in my mid back. By the time I went to this prayer meeting, ten days after the Stage 4 diagnosis was given to me, I had constant and agonizing pain in my abdomen.

After praise and worship came more talking and then a sermon longer than any I'd ever heard. At 10:00 p.m., they finally called people up for the laying on of hands and prayer. My family went with me, and a wonderful faith healer, Papa Billy, prayed over me. But nothing seemed to happen. I left the meeting in as much pain as I went into the meeting with. I rode home, confused and scared, hurting and very, very tired.

By the next day, the pain had greatly subsided. It gradually lessened throughout the weekend until it was completely gone and it has never returned! This experience was the first evidence I received of God's healing grace in my life.

## Chapter Five

# FEAR OR FAITH?

*I* was saved. I was declaring healing scriptures three times a day. I had started a consistent prayer time. I read the Bible daily. A faith healer had prayed for me and laid hands on me. And I believed with childlike faith all that I was learning in God's Word about healing, without reservations.

But it didn't take long for Satan to throw a punch. Just four days after healing hands were laid on me, and just one short week after I had invited Jesus into my life as my Lord and Savior, I went for another test – a PET scan. The purpose of the PET scan was to confirm or negate the diagnosis of metastasis of the cancer. For this particular test, I was injected with a combination radioactive/glucose substance, and then I spent the next hour being "scanned." If cancer cells were present in my lymphatic system, they would intake the glucose and glow with the radioactive substance. Well, I glowed like a Christmas tree. Everywhere the previous CT scan had located enlarged lymph nodes, the PET scan confirmed cancer activity. The actual medical report read:

There are multiple areas of moderately increased FDG-activity consistent with extensive metastatic disease.

It went on to report metastatic disease (cancer) in my left neck, diaphragm, lower abdomen near my back, and in my right groin, following the lymphatic chain to the original source of melanoma.

But the utterly amazing part about this seemingly devastating report is that I was NOT in fear! In one short week I had climbed out of the depths of despair and into God's peace that transcends all understanding (Philippians 4:7)! It didn't make sense that I wouldn't have fear. It is human nature to desperately fear pain, suffering, and death. But I had subdued my human nature and put on the nature of Jesus (Colossians 3:9-10)! I now know that fear is the opposite of faith. Since faith is of God, and fear is the opposite of faith, it clearly follows that fear is of Satan. I believe that God gave me a special gift of faith early on in my battle.

Right after the PET scan was administered, before I even had the results, my husband and I went to get a bite of lunch right in the hospital. Our total lunch bill was $6.66. Satan, the god of this world, was fighting dirty! But the name of Jesus always, always, always wins – Hallelujah! I did not go home defeated. I went home trusting God with all of my heart. I simply got out my healing declarations and proceeded to fight back!

---

*Chapter Six*

---

# LETTING GO

*F*ollowing is one of the scriptures that spoke so strongly to me during those first days and weeks of my healing journey:

*So Jesus answered and said to them, "Have faith in God. For assuredly, I say to you, whoever says to this mountain, 'Be removed and be cast into the sea,' and does not doubt in his heart, but believes that those things he says will be done, he will have whatever he says. Therefore I say to you, whatever things you ask when you pray, believe that you receive them, and you will have them.*

*"And whenever you stand praying, if you have anything against anyone, forgive him, that your Father in heaven may also forgive you your trespasses. But if you do not forgive, neither will your Father in heaven forgive your trespasses"* (Mark 11:22-26).

The first three verses show so clearly the vast importance of absolute faith that God will (not only <u>can</u>, but <u>will</u>) answer our prayers. That was the part of the scripture that I was totally and fervently standing on. But those next two scriptures nagged at me and convicted me until I turned inward and took a close look at myself. It isn't a coincidence that a scripture about forgiveness comes directly after a scripture on faith and answered prayer. The Holy Spirit clearly showed me that forgiveness is an absolute prerequisite for answered prayer, which in my case was for divine healing.

The first person in my life that the Lord led me to reconcile with was my sister. In order to explain I need to go back a bit into our history ...

As kids, I revered my big sister. I looked up to her and tried to be like her ... unsuccessfully. We were totally different people with totally different personalities. She was everything I was not; popular, outgoing, assertive, and fun! I, on the other hand, was studious and introspective and quite shy. My sister tended to react to situations with words, while I tended to react with inward thoughtfulness and stewing over the circumstances. However, as young adults we got along wonderfully. I adored my big sister.

Then we both got married. We were separated by thousands of miles since she was an Air Force wife and mother. Soon that distance was much more than just miles. When my husband and I had children, I discovered that the one thing I would not and could not accept was any criticism (even if it was justified) regarding my husband or my children. My sister, being the person she is, continuously offered her opinion and advice. Rather than communicating with her, I usually kept my thoughts and opinions inside. That was a huge mistake! I took serious offense, and gradually built a wall, and hardened my heart against my sister.

We never had a feud or a break in our relationship. I never felt unforgiveness toward her, because I honestly didn't think she'd done anything that required my forgiveness. But I was stone-cold and very distant from her. Not communicating was safe, and I was content with that.

But all of a sudden, I wasn't so safe. My body was being ravaged with a silent killer. And I was ready to fight back against cancer in any and every way possible! The Lord showed me that I needed to break down that wall that I'd built and reunite with my sister. I have learned one huge lesson in my faith journey: When the Holy Spirit prompts you to act, just do it! When you take the first step, He is there with you to give you the words and to support you every step of the way.

So that's what I did. I wrote a long letter to my sister explaining the best that I could why I'd built the invisible barricade between us. And would you believe, she had written a letter to me with almost the identical message several months prior (before the cancer diagnosis) but hadn't sent it to me.

As we truly communicated for the first time in years, I learned that I had a Spirit-filled, on-fire-for-God sister! When I needed help the most, God blessed me with a support that could only have come from Him! My sister was one of my rocks, a firm spiritual support, throughout the course of the battle that I fought.

And let me just show you one more awesome example of our God and His astonishing faithfulness. Shortly after the cancer diagnosis and the reunited relationship with my sister, she moved back to Michigan with her family. The distance was removed, both in miles and in our relationship!

Another spiritual source of strength during my battle against cancer was my husband, who has always been supportive of me in any and every endeavor of my life. But I never realized how desperately I needed his strength until I was handed a death sentence. Again, I was strongly convicted by the Lord regarding my part in our marriage relationship.

My husband is a compassionate man, always completely loving towards me, especially when I'm hurting in any way. When he saw me suffering with the life-gripping fear that attached itself to the cancer diagnosis, his heartfelt compassion flowed from the very depths of his soul. But I gravely lacked compassion. Whenever my husband was sick or hurting, I would actually feel anger toward him. It was all I could do to force myself to minister to him by taking care of him. I would be angered by his requests, his complaints, or even the time he spent resting. Well, God dealt with me about this total lack of compassion for my husband. I realized that in order for my God to act in compassion towards me, I needed to act in compassion toward others, especially my partner in marriage, united with God and by God. Again, I followed this prompting of the Holy Spirit and asked my husband and my God for forgiveness.

To this day, I begin my day in prayer by humbling myself before my mighty God; by stripping myself of worldliness, ungodliness, and self-righteousness, and asking the Lord to clothe me in the mind and heart of Jesus, with compassion to feel what He feels and to love as He loves.

Search your heart. Ask the Lord to reveal to you any areas in your life where you are harboring unforgiveness, strife, or bitterness now or from your past. You are only hurting yourself by hanging on to these death-holds. Let them go!

## Chapter Seven

# GOOD NEWS!

*M*y first good report came on March 18, almost one month after my salvation. Remember that I had previously had a CT scan that showed enlarged lymph nodes in my groin, lower abdomen, diaphragm area, and in the left side of my neck, and a PET scan had confirmed cancer activity in all four of these locations. But my doctor, guided by the wisdom of God, did not want to proceed with aggressive therapy until he had another positive biopsy of melanoma. Therefore, he ordered a fine needle biopsy of the lymph nodes in my abdomen, to be accompanied by a CT scan in order to locate the exact nodes to be biopsied.

My spiritual "attitude" was very strong. I went to the hospital armed for battle. I had my Bible, my booklet of healing scriptures, teaching tapes on healing, and a portable cassette player with headphones. When they put me in the pre-procedure area to wait, I went to work, declaring healing scriptures, reading the Word, and listening to excellent teachings on healing.

The technician and doctor who did the fine needle biopsy knew nothing of my recent medical history. After the CT scan, the doctor came to me and asked why we were attempting a fine needle biopsy, since the lymph nodes in question were so tiny, about the size of raisins. (The oncologist had reported earlier that the enlarged lymph nodes were about the size of nickels.) After I explained the series of tests I'd already undergone, and their results, he agreed to attempt the biopsy. However, even with the aid of the CT scan to show him exactly where to insert the needle, he could not draw out any cells. He attempted numerous times, but the end result was an inconclusive biopsy.

Throughout this process, I was completely filled with joy that the manifestation of God's healing was being confirmed! Their "inconclusive" diagnosis was very "conclusive" in my heart!

When my husband and I got home from the hospital that day, I opened my Bible to Isaiah 12 NIV and gave God praise with these words:

*In that day you will say: "I will praise you, O Lord … Surely God is my salvation; I will trust and not be afraid. The Lord, the Lord, is my strength and my song; he has become my salvation." With joy you will draw water from the wells of salvation. In that day you will say: "Give thanks to the Lord, call on his name; make known among the nations what he has done, and proclaim that his name is exalted. Sing to the Lord, for he has done glorious things; let this be known to all the world. Shout aloud and sing for joy, people of Zion, for great is the Holy One of Israel among you."*

## Chapter Eight

# MY HELPER

*I*n John 14 Jesus promises us the Holy Spirit. Verses 15-18 say: *"If you love Me, keep My commandments. And I will pray the Father, and He will give you another Helper, that He may abide with you forever – the Spirit of truth, whom the world cannot receive, because it neither sees Him nor knows Him; but you know Him, for He dwells with you and will be in you. I will not leave you orphans; I will come to you."*

And verses 25 and 26 repeat His promise! *"These things I have spoken to you while being present with you. But the Helper, the Holy Spirit, whom the Father will send in My name, He will teach you all things, and bring to your remembrance all things that I said to you."*

After Jesus' death and resurrection, He again told His apostles, *"Do not leave Jerusalem, but wait for the gift my Father promised, which you heard me speak about. For John baptized you with water, but in a few days you will be baptized with the Holy Spirit ...*

*"But you will receive power when the Holy Spirit comes on you; and you will be my witnesses in Jerusalem, and in all Judea and Samaria, and to the ends of the earth"* (Acts 1:4-5,8 NIV).

Acts 1 tells us that Jesus' followers did what He asked; they waited in the upper room, devoting themselves steadfastly to prayer. There were about 120 of Jesus' followers in the upper room on the day of Pentecost, including the apostles, Mary, the mother of Jesus, and His brothers!

*When the day of Pentecost came, they were all together in one place. Suddenly a sound like the blowing of a violent wind came from heaven and filled the whole house where they were sitting. They saw what seemed to be tongues of fire that separated and came to rest on each of them. All of them were filled with the Holy Spirit and began to speak in other tongues as the Spirit enabled them* (Acts 2:1-4 NIV).

In Acts 10, verses 44-48, Paul writes about when the Gentiles, whom Peter was teaching, were filled with the Holy Ghost, with the initial outward sign of speaking in tongues. Again, in Acts 19, Paul was teaching in Ephesus. These Ephesians were also baptized in the Holy Spirit and spoke in other tongues. The promise of the baptism of the Holy Spirit, made by Jesus, is available to all, just as salvation is.

I asked my Father for this gift and was baptized in the Holy Spirit on March 24, 2002. My blessed journey took a huge leap that day! *The Amplified Translation* of the Bible extends the word "Comforter" from the original Greek to mean Counselor, Helper, Intercessor, Advocate, Strengthener, and Standby! (See

John 14:16.) That's who the Holy Spirit is for all who receive Him through the baptism of the Holy Spirit!

Receiving the baptism of the Holy Spirit provides us with power from on high to become progressively more sanctified, separated from the ways of the world, and joined together with God for the purpose of doing His will. It provides us with a greater ability to receive revelation and enlightenment from the Word. It provides us with power from on high to witness to others. And it provides us with a comfort and assurance that we are never alone. We have the presence of the Holy Spirit within and upon us always, in every situation.

I began speaking in tongues when I received the baptism of the Holy Spirit. I continue to exercise this wonderful prayer language given to me by God, which enables me to pray perfect prayers to God unhindered by my limited knowledge.

I have a new life. I'm alive, totally healed physically! But even more awesome than my healing from cancer is this precious gift of the Holy Spirit. I am writing these very words with His help, with His guidance. It is with His power that I am enabled to share my testimony and the truth of His Word!

When I received the baptism of the Holy Spirit, I was only a little over a month into my faith journey. What was happening on the inside of me? The first thing that I realized was that fear was gone from my life. That all-consuming fear that had gripped me as the cancer diagnosis went from Stage 1 to Stage 3 – and then right to Stage 4 – was completely gone! In its place I had a tremendous sense of peace. I now know that it was from God, a peace that transcends all understanding (Philippians 4:7). I still had attacks of fear, but they came in short bursts, rather than the constant gripping fear I had originally experienced.

The second huge change in my life resulted from a revelation of my sanctification. "Sanctification" means to be holy, to be separated from the ways of the world and from sin, to be set apart for God, to strive to be like Him, and to seek His righteousness and fellowship with all of your heart. Sanctification comes as a result of being born again. The baptism of the Holy Spirit heightened my awareness of the Holy Spirit's indwelling presence, which stirred me up with a deep desire to truly live the Word! With this progressive revelation of sanctification, I experienced several immediate changes in my life.

- ✞ I had an intense desire to spend time with the Lord, in prayer, in praise and worship, and in reading His Word.
- ✞ When I read the Word, it was opened to me, like a code being broken. Prior to my salvation and subsequent infilling with the Holy Spirit, I had great difficulty reading the Bible and simply didn't understand much of what it said. After the infilling of the Holy Spirit, the Word opened up to me with even greater clarity, and continues to open to me in new ways, with new revelations and deeper understanding.
- ✞ I wanted to talk about God, His Word, and His work in my life constantly and was filled with joy whenever I was talking about Him.
- ✞ I was strongly convicted with some of the things that I had previously enjoyed in my life, like trashy novels,

videos, and using crude language. I remember spring cleaning that year. I threw away my collection of what I called "smut novels" and a whole collection of trashy videos. I didn't want them in my house, and I wouldn't even give them away. If they weren't good for me, I certainly didn't want to give them to someone else.

This was an important stage in the sanctification process in my life. I am in awe of my God. All I did was say "yes" to Him, ask Him into my life, and open my heart in surrender to Him. But He is so faithful! He came right on in and began filling me up with Him, and with His goodness there simply wasn't enough room for the junk! Like my pastor says, "When you get new furniture, you don't set it on top of your old furniture ... you get rid of the old stuff!" That's what sanctification is! You can't do it on your own, but with the Holy Spirit within you, it is a joy to clean house spiritually!

## Chapter Nine

# MY HUSBAND'S NEW BIRTH

*M*y husband, Kent, is an incredible man. I've already mentioned his compassionate heart. From the day we started dating until now (twenty-seven plus years of marriage) my husband has treated me as though I'm more precious than gold. He solidly supported me through the initial days of my battle with cancer. But after he received Jesus as his Lord and Savior, he became a source of spiritual strength. He became one with me in my spiritual fight against the evil of cancer.

Kent and I had begun planning a winter Caribbean vacation with our daughter and our niece in October, before I had received the melanoma diagnosis. We did not cancel our travel plans when the doctor gave us the bad report. Since 9/11 had terrorized our nation the previous fall, we had purchased traveler's insurance with our vacation reservations, just in case we would opt not to travel in April. That insurance turned out to be a huge blessing. We decided to hold onto the reservations and cancel them if necessary right before the trip. But it wasn't necessary! The doctors were still in the middle of the staging process, and they agreed that a Caribbean vacation was excellent medicine for me! God's plans are so perfect!

Kent absolutely loves the Caribbean. This particular trip was our seventh trip to Jamaica, where the average daily temperature year round is 85, and the water temperature is 80. My husband is a scuba diver and is in awe of the beauty of the Caribbean Sea. We had previously talked about praying together for his salvation, but he wasn't quite ready to surrender. He wanted to wait and receive Jesus as his Lord and Savior in the Caribbean, his favorite place in the world!

Early one morning in Jamaica, I was awakened by a sound like a pebble or a branch hitting the window. It repeatedly tapped and tapped. I remember saying to the Lord, "Okay, okay, Lord, I'm awake and I'll get up and spend some time with You!" I went to the sitting room adjacent to the bedroom to have my morning time in fellowship with my Father.

As I was in prayer, I had a vision of a huge rock, surrounded by rays of light. Then the Lord led me to Psalm 62. Verses 5-8 say, *My soul, wait only upon God and silently submit to Him; for my hope and expectation are from Him. He only is my Rock and my Salvation; He is my Defense and my Fortress, I shall not be moved. With God rests my salvation and my glory; He is my Rock of unyielding strength and impenetrable hardness, and my refuge is in God! Trust in, lean on, rely on, and have confidence in Him at all times, you people; pour out your hearts before Him. God is a refuge for us (a fortress and a high tower). Selah [pause, and calmly think of that]!* (AMP).

As I was meditating on this Word from God, and the loud and clear message it contains regarding salvation, Kent woke up and came into the sitting room. I shared my vision and Psalm 62 with him and asked him if he'd like to pray for his salvation. He said "yes," and we prayed together. My husband asked Jesus into his life, to wash away his iniquities, to heal him body, mind, and spirit, to redeem his life from destruction, to be the Lord of his life, to lead him, to guide him, and to direct the path of his life. My husband stepped into his eternal life on April 5, 2002!

Kent is a new man. *Therefore, if anyone is in Christ, he is a new creation; old things have passed away; behold, all things have become new* (2 Corinthians 5:17). Kent had been attending church and was under excellent teaching of the Word, but after receiving his salvation, and shortly thereafter the baptism of the Holy Spirit, his desire to grow in his Christian maturity increased exponentially!

Kent has always been an incredible man and husband. But now he is a mighty ambassador for Christ. We pray together, believe together, worship together, read and study the Word together, share our "God incidences" with one another, discuss the Word and the Lord's work in our lives, and live our lives together for the Lord!

(By the way, on the morning of Kent's salvation as we left the room to start our day and Kent's eternal life in the Caribbean sun, I stopped outside of our window to look and see what was causing the tapping. But there were only ferns in the garden … another God incident!)

## Chapter Ten

# SEEKING WISDOM

*I* love the *Amplified Translation* of Matthew 7:7-8: *Keep on asking and it will be given you; keep on seeking and you will find; keep on knocking [reverently] and [the door] will be opened to you. For everyone who keeps on asking receives; and he who keeps on seeking finds; and to him who keeps on knocking, [the door] will be opened.*

I was scheduled for another PET scan on April 19, two months after the initial Stage 4 diagnosis of melanoma. To those of you who are going through a battle with cancer, or have a loved one with cancer, you know that doctors do not waste time before starting cancer treatment. But after the inconclusive fine needle biopsy, my doctor was not yet ready to proceed with treatment without more definite confirmation of the cancer. He ordered the second PET scan to do just that.

What he didn't know was that I had been receiving the absolute best cancer treatment for two solid months. I'd been declaring healing scriptures over the cancer. I'd been devouring the nutrition of the Word. I'd been praising and worshipping the Lord, and spending time daily in fervent prayer. My specific prayer for this test was for a good report, but I was also seeking godly wisdom and direction regarding the results of the PET scan. Just as Matthew 7:7 directs, I asked and kept on asking.

The day before the test I was attacked by Satan with monumental fear. I came home from work that day, went into my bedroom with my Bible, knelt down and cried out to the Lord in anguish. Once again, the Lord was there to comfort me and to give me strength. I opened my Bible randomly, and five words were underlined on the page I opened to: *Be not afraid, only believe* (Mark 5:36 KJV). Just as Jesus directed Jairus, *"Be not afraid, only believe,"* when Jairus was told that his daughter had died, He was also directing me that day in my bedroom.

In order to receive healing, you must have faith, and fear is the opposite of faith. Fear is a destroyer. Faith is a restorer. I went to church that evening and talked to Jenny about the fear. She immediately said, "You are not leaving tonight with fear," and she took me to a pastor for prayer. He shared another powerful scripture with me, 2 Timothy 1:7: *For God has not given us a spirit of fear, but of power and of love and of a sound mind.* And he prayed with me. The support of my husband, Jenny – my spiritual mentor, and my church family was critical, especially when I was dealing with fear!

I went in for the PET scan with a magnificent peace. When they took me back for the radioactive/glucose injection, I had my Bible with me. However, I was not allowed to hold it to read, since I needed to lie completely still in order for the injection to flow evenly to all parts of my body. But they couldn't stop me from praying! I was so anointed with the Holy Spirit that I could tangibly feel Him throughout my body. The actual PET scan lasted about an hour, during which I meditated on and spoke the Word, and I prayed. My husband, my constant source of support, was with me.

I didn't expect the test results for several days, as I had learned was routine procedure. But to our surprise, the doctor who analyzed the PET scan called us back into the office immediately after the scan was completed. She told us that this PET scan confirmed the initial diagnosis; melanoma was active in lymph nodes in my neck, diaphragm area, and in my lower abdomen.

When she initially gave us this news, fear immediately started raging inside me. But then, just as suddenly as the fear had attacked, it began to recede. The godly wisdom that I had prayed for began to ignite. The Lord gave me excellent questions to ask, to dig deeper into the seemingly bad report.

The doctor spent a long time with Kent and me. What we learned through the in-depth discussion with the doctor is that the PET scan also measures the <u>degree</u> of glucose intake from the cancer. If the degree of intake on the second PET scan was less than on the first PET scan, it would show a reduction in cancer activity. However, since the first PET scan was done at the University of Michigan Cancer Institute and the second one was done at the Karmanos Cancer Institute, there was no way of comparing these crucial numbers. Another piece of good news was that the second PET scan did NOT show cancer activity in the lymph node in my groin, the area which initially tested positive for melanoma through a fine needle biopsy.

At any rate, I went home with confidence that God was doing a good work within my body. And I was filled with peace, not fear.

The next morning during my prayer time, God revealed another *rhema* word to me: Philippians 1:6,12 NIV: *Being confident of this, that he who began a good work in you will carry it on to completion until the day of Christ Jesus . . . And what has happened to me has really served to advance the gospel!*

The same confidence I felt the day before, the absolute knowing that God was doing a good work in my body, was confirmed through the Word of God! God is so good!

## Chapter Eleven

# CHOICES

$\mathcal{I}$ went to see my oncologist the following week. It was time to make a decision and to proceed with treatment. He gave me three options.

Option 1: Do nothing. However, my doctor strongly discouraged this option. Melanoma was clearly indicated through the most recent PET scan. According to my doctor, the melanoma was incurable, and without treatment I had only six to nine months to live. (This was the first time I had heard this prognosis.)

Option 2: Treat the cancer as if it were in stage 3, contained within the lymph nodes in my groin. In that case, I would have the lymph node dissection initially recommended, followed by a year of interferon treatment. But again, if the cancer had indeed spread throughout my lymph node system as the PET scan indicated, I would not be adequately fighting the disease. When I discussed with the doctor that the most recent PET scan hadn't even shown cancer activity in my groin, he seemed to totally disregard those results, saying that the cancer was definitely there, that it wouldn't just "go away" without treatment.

Option 3: Have exploratory surgery to actually look carefully into my abdominal cavity, remove a good sampling of lymph nodes, and determine the staging with absolute accuracy. At that point, if melanoma was pathologically confirmed, the oncologist recommended aggressive chemo-imunotherapy, to the extent that I would be hospitalized for a week at a time for the treatments, and would undergo a minimum of three rounds of chemo-imunotherapy. This is the option he recommended.

Kent and I told him we needed to pray about the options, and discuss them before making a decision. As we were leaving, he warned us to make the decision quickly since time was critical.

Yes, time was critical! But God's timing is always perfect! It just so happened that Charles Capps was coming to our church that very weekend. He is the man of faith who compiled the healing scriptures into the booklet that I had been confessing three times a day since February 19!

I spent extensive time that weekend in prayer. I had learned that when we need to make a decision that is not directly revealed in the Word, praying in the Spirit will bring direction to our spirit. So I prayed in tongues throughout the weekend, seeking peace regarding one of the three options which my doctor had proposed.

Kent and I went to the Charles Capps services Sunday morning and again on Sunday evening. Charles Capps taught about the prayer of faith, about the power of confessing the Word over circumstances, and about believing without wavering.

I received a major revelation that day. I had been believing that God was in the process of healing me, not that I <u>was healed</u>! But the truth is, Jesus had already provided for my healing when He suffered and died for me! I changed my confessions from that day onward, believing that I was totally healed and that the cancer was completely destroyed!

I made my decision for medical intervention. I decided to go with Option 3 – exploratory surgery. I believed that the medical confirmation of my healing would be a huge testimony, first to give glory to the Lord, but also to show my family and friends the power of God! I had peace with my decision, as did Kent. I called the oncologist on Monday morning, April 29, with our decision. I was referred to a surgeon, and the surgery was scheduled for June 18, five long months after my journey had begun!

## Chapter Twelve

# MY YOUTH IS RENEWED
# AS THE EAGLE'S

When the surgery was about three weeks ahead of me, I had an incredible experience. I was driving home from work, confessing healing scriptures over the cancer. I had just confessed the following: You have forgiven all of my iniquities. You have healed my body of disease. You have redeemed my life from destruction. You have satisfied my mouth with good things so that my youth is renewed as the eagle's. (This is not a direct quotation from the Bible, but a paraphrased confession based on Psalm 103:2-3,5.)

I stopped to meditate on this scripture, on all that Jesus had done for me when He took my sins and the effects of those sins to the cross. He forgave all of my sins. He healed my body of cancer. He redeemed my life from destruction, and provided me with eternal life! And then I prayed this prayer. I said, "Father God, I praise You and I thank You for taking such good care of me. I believe with every fiber of my being that You have healed my body of cancer. But I can't see inside my body, and I could really use some confirmation. Lord, show me that my youth is truly renewed as the eagle's. Show me an eagle!"

Now, I need to say that I had never before asked God so specifically for confirmation of prayer. Our heavenly Father loves us so much! He meets us right where we are! Just as an earthly father wants to reassure his kids when they are in need, my Father is always there to reassure and to comfort me! The last part of Psalm 103, verse 4, that was not included in my original confession, is: You crown me with loving-kindness and tender mercies. And that's exactly what my awesome God did!

When I arrived at home, Kent was cooking dinner. I walked into the kitchen to put down my stuff, and the first thing that I saw was an eagle soaring across the entire television screen. I stood there in awe, silently praising God for His goodness, but in the back of my mind I was questioning if this was really the confirmation I had asked for. After all, it wasn't a <u>real</u> eagle! I think God may have said, "Cindy, just trust Me, okay?" But God, being so incredibly good, reconfirmed my renewed youth over and over again within the next few days.

We left for the cottage that evening for Memorial Day weekend. I watched for an eagle throughout the weekend, but it was rainy and cold so I stayed inside by the fire most of the time. On Sunday morning we all went to church, and the first hymn was "On Eagle's Wings." Confirmation #2! Again, I was overcome with praise of my awesome God!

That afternoon my parents came to the cottage for a visit. They have lived in the general vicinity of our cottage their whole lives. I asked my dad if he'd seen any eagles around the lake lately. He told me that he'd never seen an eagle in that area.

A few short minutes later, the kids came exploding into the house. They had been out on the speedboat, braving the weather. My oldest son, then twenty-two years old, was so excited he was almost shouting, "Mom, you can't believe what just happened. We were out on the boat, and an eagle soared right over us, dove into the water and caught a fish, and landed on our island to eat it!"

At that point, I was overcome with the revelation of the loving-kindness of my Father. He had given me exactly what I had asked, a real live eagle to confirm that my youth was indeed renewed! I shared my prayer and God's answer with my family. My healing was confirmed. I had received the total manifestation of my healing!

But God wasn't done quite yet. That evening, I picked up the book that I'd been reading, *Just Enough LIGHT for the Step I'm On, Trusting God in the Tough Times*, by Stormie Omartian. The scripture at the beginning of the chapter I was about to read was,

> *Those who wait on the Lord shall renew their strength;*
> *They shall mount up with wings like eagles,*
> *They shall run and not be weary,*
> *They shall walk and not faint.*
> Isaiah 40:31

I had never read that particular scripture before. Confirmation #4! Praise God!!!

I got home from the cottage on Monday night and was going through the mail. I had received literally hundreds of cards from my friends and family throughout the ordeal with cancer. But this particular card was the only one of all of those hundreds with a picture of a soaring eagle and the following verse:

*When you come to the edge of all the light you know,*
*And are about to step off into the darkness of the unknown,*
*Faith is knowing one of two things will happen:*
*There will be something solid to stand on*
*Or You will be taught how to fly.*
*By Barbara J. Winter*

*May you be guided by the light of faith every step of the way.*

God answered my prayer by confirming my healing with not one, but <u>five</u> eagle experiences! He is so faithful, and He has continuously crowned me with loving-kindness and tender mercies!

A couple of weeks later, I was sharing this testimony with one of our dear friends at the lake. She said that on Memorial Day weekend, there was an eagle around our island all weekend. They were all watching it in awe, not even realizing that it was such a huge sign to me from my Abba Father.

We still have an eagle that frequently perches on a tree right outside of our cottage. I'm often the first one up, desiring my private time with the Lord. What a blessing it is to open the door to a new day of life, and to see the eagle He has blessed me with lift his wings and soar out over the lake and beyond!

## Chapter Thirteen

# UNITY

The weekend before my scheduled exploratory surgery, my sister and I went to Steubenville, Ohio, to a Charismatic healing conference at the Franciscan University. At this point, I had completely surrendered myself to the Lord, and was attending a new church where I was being richly nourished spiritually. I had been brought up in the Catholic church, where I had received a wonderful foundation of faith. However, in my Catholic upbringing, I was lacking knowledge in the importance of surrendering my life to the Lord and establishing a relationship with Him. I was not aware of the power of the Holy Spirit. I did not know that healing is available for all those who believe.

In the days and weeks before the conference, I prayed for the following:

1. That the conference would be a spiritually fulfilling experience.
2. That I would see positive aspects in the Catholic church where I was feeling quite negative.
3. To be bold with my sister; to communicate with her about God, my faith, and my testimonies.

4. To pray with my sister and to form a strong spiritual bond.

5. To have great expectation of the manifestation of God's healing power. To believe in the healing of my body with my whole heart, without wavering, and to accept healing in my body, mind, and spirit.

God answered each aspect of my prayer in a mighty way. The conference was outstanding. The teaching that went forth regarding healing in this Charismatic Catholic Conference was in total agreement with the teaching I had been receiving through my new church. I took the following notes at the Steubenville conference.

✟ The age of miracles is now, not just in the past!

✟ The Catholic church knows and believes in the power of healing.

✟ Healing is for everyone. As far as God is concerned, He has already provided for our healing. There's no example in the Bible where Jesus said, "No, I won't heal you." If we don't receive healing, we need to look within ourselves rather than blaming God.

✟ Seek first the Kingdom of God, and all else will follow.

✟ Forgiveness is one of the absolute conditions for reception of healing.

✟ Fear and anxiety are the opposite of faith.

✟ Fear is an implicit denial of the redemption of Jesus Christ. Living in faith is knowing who you are and to Whom you belong.

✟ There is authority in the name of Jesus.

✟ Turn away from the world. The world is ruled by the prince of darkness. We are in spiritual warfare against Satan. In order to resist Satan, we must stand on the Word of God. Protection requires obedience to the Word.

✟ Sanctification is your weapon against evil.

✟ If you do not agree with the Word of God, it is not the Word of God that must change, it's you.

✟ Praising God, especially in tongues, is powerful.

✟ Praying in tongues is very, very important. In Acts 2, 120 believers all prayed in tongues.

✟ When we pray, we should claim the blood of Jesus Christ, the summary of all redemption. When we receive Jesus as our Lord and Savior, we are forgiven, washed clean, and receive the mercy of God. We come out of darkness into the kingdom of light. The kingdom of Satan was overturned by the power of the cross. The law of the Spirit of life has made us free from the law of sin and death!

The conference was Spirit-filled, with the gifts of the Spirit being manifested through the gift of tongues, prophecies, and healings. We spent hours in true praise and worship, pouring out our love to God with total abandonment, not thinking about the person on our left or our right, but only upward to our heavenly Father. The teaching of the Word was rich with truth, and the celebration of Mass was truly alive. The first two parts of my prayer had been clearly answered. The conference truly <u>was</u> a spiritually fulfilling experience, and I could clearly see positive aspects in the Catholic church where I was feeling quite negative prior to the conference.

My sister had been baptized in the Holy Spirit years earlier, but didn't understand that she needed to give her voice to the Lord in order to pray in tongues. The first morning at the conference, my sister and I got up early to go to the chapel and pray. There was one other woman in the chapel. After a time of private prayer, this woman approached me and said that she was being strongly led by the Spirit to pray with my sister and me. The woman and I began praying in tongues. Soon my sister gave her voice over to the Holy Spirit, and was absolutely fluent in tongues. She was ecstatic! She went to the conference to support me, to stand by me through a trial in my life, to believe with me for my healing … but she also received a wonderful gift!

More of my initial prayer was so wonderfully answered that weekend! I was bold with my sister. I communicated with her about God, my faith, and my testimonies. I prayed fervently with my sister, and we formed a strong spiritual bond.

In the years since our Steubenville experience, we have remained close prayer partners and spiritual friends, but we have also experienced division over the specifics and the differences in our faith. My prayer today for my sister and me, as well as for the entire Church of Jesus Christ, is that we would be in unity; that we would focus on our common beliefs, and not the differences of our beliefs.

As Paul tells the Colossians, *And have clothed yourselves with the new [spiritual self], which is [ever in the process of being] renewed and remolded into [fuller and more perfect knowledge upon] knowledge after the image (the likeness) of Him Who created it. [In this new creation all distinctions vanish.] There is no room for and there can be neither Greek nor Jew, circumcised nor uncircumcised, [nor difference between nations whether alien] barbarians or Scythians [who are the most savage of all], nor slave or free man; but Christ is all and in all [everything and everywhere, to all men, without distinction of person]* (Colossians 3:10-11 AMP).

The manifestations of the gifts of healings were so awesome at the conference! Multitudes of people were touched by the Spirit and healed. Frequently throughout the weekend, a minister of the Word would receive a word of knowledge regarding a specific need for healing (such as blindness, arthritis, etc.). A word of knowledge is a supernatural manifestation of specific knowledge in the mind of God concerning past or present situations. The priest would then call those people forth for laying on of hands.

At one point, a word of knowledge came forth regarding being healed of cancer (not a need for healing, but rather an invitation to publicly praise God for healing already received!). I acknowledged my healing, standing and praising Jesus for taking the stripes and dying for me so that I could be healed! The last part of my Steubenville prayer was answered. I had a mighty expectation of the manifestation of God's healing power. I believed in the healing of my body with my whole heart, without wavering, and I <u>accepted</u> Jesus' total and complete healing of my body, soul, and spirit.

## Chapter Fourteen

# A GREAT REPORT!

*I* am in awe as I look back at the sequence of events from the initial cancer diagnosis to the great report that I'm about to share; how I was on a downward spiral with one bad report after another, until my new faith journey began. At that point, I started the climb back uphill, finally reaching the summit on June 18, 2002.

I was originally scheduled for an early morning surgery, but the day prior to the surgery, the hospital called to reschedule for the early afternoon. The schedule change was actually a blessing, because I had all morning to prepare spiritually. I started my day reading the Word, confessing healing scriptures over myself, and praying. Kent and I took a nice bike ride on that beautiful spring morning. Then he mowed the grass while I worked in my garden.

I watered the flowers, pulled weeds, and then decided to prune the dead lilacs out of the bush. As I was pruning, I started to see those dead blooms as dead cancer. With every cut of the pruning shears, I said, "Cancer, you are dead, you are gone, you are dried up and cut out of my body." I remember angrily hacking away at death, at the lies of Satan and his destruction. The tears were coursing down my cheeks as I tangibly chopped out death, pruning it from the living tree.

I don't remember many details from the remainder of that day, until I woke up in the recovery room. Kent was standing over me with this huge smile, telling me there was absolutely no cancer! Tidal waves of relief flooded over me. There simply aren't words to describe the praise that I had for my God at that moment. I wanted to sob and cry out my praise, but my tummy hurt too much!

After my husband spent some more time with me, I sent him off to get some dinner. But before he left, I had him help me put on a headset so I could worship the Lord through music. One song in particular led me into the Lord's presence on that joyous evening. Here are the lyrics:

> *My Jesus, My Savior*
> *Lord, there is none like You.*
> *All of my days I want to praise*
> *The wonders of Your mighty love.*
> *My Comfort, my Shelter*
> *Tower of refuge and strength*
> *Let every breath, all that I am*
> *Never cease to worship You!*
> *Shout to the Lord all the earth let us sing.*
> *Power and majesty praise to the King.*
> *Mountains bow down and the seas will roar*
> *At the sound of Your name.*
> *I sing for joy at the sound of Your name*
> *Forever I'll love You, forever I'll stand.*
> *Nothing compares to the promise I have in You!*

CCLI #1360011
Darlene Zschech, © 1993 Hillsongs, Australia

I had a wonderful surgeon. He was always very positive and encouraging. The day after surgery, he told Kent and me that he had done a visual exam during the exploratory surgery, and he was very impressed with my abdominal cavity! (What kind of a compliment is that?) He said that it looked perfect. He had taken a sampling of lymph nodes and had done an initial frozen biopsy right in the operating room. These results were all negative for melanoma; however, the actual pathology report would take a few days to get. He had also done another fine needle biopsy of the lymph node in my groin that had originally tested positive for melanoma. Again, we didn't have the final results, but he said that there was a lot of fluid consistent with a cyst, as opposed to cancer, which was a good sign.

I got the pathology report a few days later. **All the lymph nodes were negative for melanoma!** If there were even one cancer cell within them, the pathology report would have been positive. I absolutely did NOT have cancer in my abdominal cavity!

**The fine needle biopsy of the lymph node in my groin also came back negative for melanoma!** Of course, I was totally and completely healed! Jesus died for my healing, and I received it! Hallelujah!

By now my oncologist was quite perplexed. Multiple CT scans and PET scans had so clearly pointed to metastasis of melanoma throughout my lymphatic system ... but now there appeared to be no cancer in those very areas! At my follow-up appointment, he suggested we now go ahead with Stage 3 treatment; the lymph node dissection in my right groin, followed by a year of interferon treatment. But Kent and I were totally confident that my healing was complete … Stage 0! My doctor simply wasn't so sure. He again reiterated that cancer doesn't just go away, and that the fine needle biopsy wasn't an absolute negative, because it was only a sampling of cells. So we made a slight compromise.

I agreed to another surgery, to remove just the one lymph node in question. If the frozen biopsy in the operating room came back negative, that's all I wanted them to do. If the frozen biopsy was positive, the surgeon could go ahead with the complete lymph node dissection (which would involve removing a section of tissue containing all of the lymph nodes in that area of my body). I was also scheduled to have a wide local excision of the original site of the melanoma on my buttock, in order to check all the surrounding tissue for melanoma.

This surgery was scheduled one month after the first surgery, on July 19. I was believing for another good report, confessing my healing scriptures, and growing stronger and stronger in the maturity of my faith every day. On the day of the surgery, I was adamant that I would not take one pill or accept an IV until I'd talked to the surgeon personally. I wanted to make absolutely sure that he knew what steps to take during the surgery. But he was as positive as I, believing that the original cancerous lymph node would be negative for melanoma.

And of course, it was! When I came out of surgery, Kent was again there waiting for me. But this time he was ready to take me home right then and there! I didn't even need to spend a night in the hospital, since the simple excision of the lymph node was so minor. The frozen biopsy was negative, as was the final pathology report from both the lymph node and the margins test from my buttock. There was one interesting twist to the negative report from the lymph node in my groin. It seems that rather than a cancerous lymph node, I had a small hernial sac! (Since my own healing, I've been witness to several other healings where a terminal diagnosis suddenly and curiously changed, which I will share in Part 2 of *A Blessed Journey*.)

No further treatment was required, no chemotherapy, no interferon, nothing! I was declared cancer free!

My doctor could not explain the whole ordeal I had experienced, but I explained it to him! I simply told him that my awesome God had healed me! It was a miracle. At that point, I saw him smile for the first time ever and he said, "I like miracles!" to which I answered, "So do I!"

*Chapter Fifteen*

# THE BATTLE CONTINUES

*I*f it is not God's will for people to be sick and suffer in order to "teach" them an important life lesson, then why in the world do people get sick? The answer is hidden in the question! It is because they are <u>in the world</u>, and the god of this world (Satan) is the cause of all evil, including sickness and pain. I didn't know much about Satan before the cancer. I knew <u>of</u> him, I just didn't have any comprehension of the active role he plays in our world. First, let me share a few scriptures that show that Satan does indeed have authority over the world.

### LUKE 4:5-6

*Then the devil, taking Him (Jesus) up on a high mountain, showed Him all the kingdoms of the world in a moment of time. And the devil said to Him, "All this authority I will give You, and their glory; for this has been delivered to me, and I give it to whomever I wish."*

Satan was given authority over our world with the fall of man in the Garden of Eden.

## 2 CORINTHIANS 4:4 AMP

*For the god of this world has blinded the unbelievers' minds [that they should not discern the truth], preventing them from seeing the illuminating light of the Gospel of the glory of Christ (the Messiah), Who is the Image and Likeness of God.*

Notice that the god of this world (Satan) has blinded the minds of unbelievers. But, hallelujah, look what the Word has to say about believers!

## COLOSSIANS 1:13-14 AMP

*[The Father] has delivered and drawn us to Himself out of the control and the dominion of darkness and has transferred us into the kingdom of the Son of His love, in Whom we have our redemption through His blood, [which means] the forgiveness of our sins.*

## COLOSSIANS 2:13-15 NIV

*When you were dead in your sins and in the uncircumcision of your sinful nature, God made you alive with Christ. He forgave us all our sins, having canceled the written code, with its regulations, that was against us and that stood opposed to us; he took it away, nailing it to the cross. And having disarmed the powers and authorities, he made a public spectacle of them, triumphing over them by the cross.*

The process of being made alive with Christ involves completely and totally surrendering your life to Jesus as your Lord and Savior. If you have done this, YOU HAVE AUTHORITY over Satan, over sin, over cancer, over any sickness or pain, over fear, over worry, over eternal damnation ... through the blood of our Savior, which has washed us clean! We are given the name of Jesus for authority. The devil has no power over the believer unless we give it to him!

## LUKE 10:19

*Behold, I give you the authority to trample on serpents and scorpions, and over all the power of the enemy, and nothing shall by any means hurt you.*

Satan is the author of sickness and disease. Satan put cancer in my body. I allowed him to do that through ignorance. I had no relationship with God. I did not seek God <u>first</u> in my life. He was way down the list of my priorities. My children and my husband were at the top of my list, closely followed by my extended family and friends, my career, material things, and then way down on my priority list was God. Even though I religiously went to church every single Sunday, I never poured out my love to my Father with songs of worship and praise, and I didn't attempt to take away the lesson from the sermon and apply it to my life. But I believed that I was a good person. I believed that I kept all of God's commandments. I was moral and ethical. But I was not a child of God. I had not freely surrendered my life to God ... until I was faced with the death sentence.

Before the cancer, I hadn't even known Satan was in my life. But, boy oh boy, did I ever get to know Satan after I received my salvation! Now that I had authority, Satan came on the attack around every bend in the road.

As soon as the cancer diagnosis was given to me, even when the doctors thought it was very minute and totally curable, I started having symptoms.

I am a learning consultant and work in an elementary school. A few weeks after the initial diagnosis, I was administering MEAP tests, Michigan's version of proficiency testing. As I monitored the kids, I was gripped with pain in my lower back, and with a fear even more painful. I left the testing session close to hysterics, crying uncontrollably, called a nurse at the University of Michigan Cancer Institute, and described the symptoms to her. She proceeded to calm me down with her assurance that melanoma would not spread that fast, and that it was very common for patients to have psychosomatic symptoms with a cancer diagnosis. (That's because Satan is hard at work!)

I remember one of the worst days I experienced. I had received the Stage 4 diagnosis, but was newly saved, and had just started my faith journey. Satan, the author of death and dying, was fighting dirty. I didn't sleep, couldn't eat, and felt as if I were in a vacuum, with life being sucked out of me at breakneck speed.

On this particular day, I called in sick, because I simply couldn't face the day. I remember sitting in my prayer chair, staring into nothingness. But I wasn't praying. I couldn't. My husband knew I was deep in despair, and this is one time he was sucked down with me. He knelt in front of me, put his head in my lap, and sobbed and sobbed. I didn't even shed a tear. I was numb.

Later that day, I called the oncologist. I had an appointment for later in the week, but I told his nurse that I really needed to come in sooner; that the cancer was growing rapidly, I could feel it, and I was terrified I would die before the appointment.

Later that day, I forced myself to go to the bookstore, and buy several books about cancer and their treatments. When I opened them to read, more waves of fear wrapped around my life, trying to squeeze life out of me. I tried to do some cancer research on the Internet, but that was the worst of all. Fear is the opposite of faith. Satan was feeding me every morsel of fear food he could find. And I was eating it up.

But thank God, my husband, my sister, my church and fellow believers were there to support me, to teach me, to pray with me, to walk with me in faith. And God simply carried me, the way a father carries a child! Within a week or two of my salvation, the fear lifted and left me with an incredible peace.

The fear would occasionally attack me, but I knew how to take authority over the fear and drive it back. Just as I confessed healing scriptures over the cancer in my body, I also confessed scriptures over the fear, and exercised my authority as a believer over Satan and his attacks. Here are some of my "weapons of defense." (All of the following scriptures are paraphrased confessions based on the Scriptures noted. They are not direct quotations from the Bible.)

✞ **Ephesians 6:10-18** - I am strong in the Lord and in His mighty power. I put on the full armor of God so that I can take my stand against the devil's schemes. For my struggle is not against flesh and blood (or cancer) but against the rulers, against the authorities, against the powers of this dark world and against the spiritual forces of evil in the heavenly realms. Therefore, I put on the full armor of God, so that when the day of evil comes, I may be able to stand my ground, and after I have done everything, to stand. I stand firm then, with the belt of truth buckled around my waist, with the breastplate of righteousness in place, and with my feet fitted with the readiness that comes from the gospel of peace. In addition to all this, I take up the shield of faith, with which I can extinguish all the flaming arrows of the evil one. I take the helmet of salvation and the sword of the Spirit, which is the Word of God. And I pray in the Spirit on all occasions with all kinds of prayers and requests.

✝ **Isaiah 54:17** - No weapon that the enemy sets up against me will prosper today, because God is my defense!

✝ **James 4:7** - I am submitted to God, and the devil flees from me because I resist him in the name of Jesus.

✝ **Luke 10:19, 1 John 3:8** - I have authority over all the power of the enemy, and I destroy all of his works in Jesus' name!

I soon discovered a pattern of Satan's strongest attacks. He would attack me before a big test (such as a CT or PET scan), and he would attack me after a good report.

I had just received my all clear from the doctor. It was after my second surgery. The exploratory surgery and lymph node excision had all come back negative for melanoma. I was declared cancer free, with no need for further treatment. That's when the attack came.

You see, the original scans showed melanoma in my groin, my lower and upper abdomen, and in my neck. The surgeries had confirmed that I had no cancer in my groin or in my abdomen, but I had no such confirmation regarding the melanoma detected by the CT and PET scans in my neck. That's when I started having symptoms in my neck. My neck hurt. I constantly poked and prodded my lymph nodes and felt hard little nodules. I was consistently declaring my healing scriptures, but still worrying about the nagging symptoms. These symptoms continued for months. I had the doctor check my neck, and he said that the lymph nodes in my neck were just fine. But the symptoms kept haunting me.

Then God gave me a *rhema* word that enabled me to conquer Satan's relentless lies. He gave me the word in my sleep. When I awoke on this particular day, in the autumn following my all-clear surgeries, "Deuteronomy 1" was in my mind, and it would not go away, kind of like a melody stuck in my head. I had never read the book of Deuteronomy. In fact, I hadn't read much of the Old Testament at all. But this word from God saved my life.

The book of Deuteronomy was written by Moses near the end of his life. In this book, Moses restated and summarized the previous four books of the Old Testament, and exhorted Israel to retain and obey the previously revealed truth of God as already given in His absolute and unchanging Word.

The first chapter of Deuteronomy tells of when the Israelites were in the desert, and the Lord instructed them, through Moses, to take possession of the hill country of the Amorites, encouraging them not to be afraid or discouraged. Twelve men were sent to spy out the land before moving ahead with God's plan for them. But even though the twelve came back with some of the fruit of the land and reported, "It is a good land that the Lord our God is giving us," the people were still unwilling to go and take possession of the land. They rebelled against the command of the Lord. They grumbled and complained, believing that the Amorites were stronger and taller, worried that the cities were large with strong walls.

But Moses told them, *"Do not be terrified; do not be afraid of them. The Lord your God, who is going before you, will fight for you, as he did for you in Egypt, before your very eyes, and in the desert. There you saw how the Lord your God carried you, as a father carries his son, all the way you went until you reached this place. In spite of this, you did not trust in the Lord your God, who went ahead of you on your journey, in fire by night and in a cloud by day, to search out places for you to camp and to show you the way you should go"* (Deuteronomy 1:29-32 NIV).

The Lord was angry at their grumbling and disbelief. Moses conveyed God's anger to them, and then they replied, *"We have sinned against the Lord. We will go up and fight, as the Lord our God commanded us"* (v. 41). But the Lord told Moses not to go, because He would not be with them, and they would be defeated by the Amorites. They went anyway and were defeated in that battle.

As I read and reread and meditated on this chapter of Deuteronomy, the Lord revealed to me the parallel between the Israelites and my own life. First, the Lord had allowed the seven plagues upon Egypt, which in and of themselves were mighty signs and wonders. Then the Lord delivered the Israelites out of slavery, constantly protecting them and providing for their needs. He parted the Red Sea for them, allowing it to close over their enemies. He fed them manna from heaven, and then quail when they were complaining of the manna. He gave them water from a rock. He showed them their way with a cloud that moved when they should move and stopped when they should stop. But still they grumbled and complained with doubt, fear, and unbelief.

And here I was, doing the same thing. God had given me my miracle. He had confirmed my healing, first through His majestic eagle, then through the negative pathology reports of melanoma, both in my abdomen and in my groin. But I was still in fear, doubting and not believing God's perfect healing. Remember that in the Old Testament event, the Israelites lost their battle against the Amorites. It was very possible that if I continued in my unbelief, I would lose my battle against cancer. But God is so good! When we miss it from one direction, He shows us another one! I recognized this warning, loud and clear! I took the words from this scripture, and added them to my spiritual warfare arsenal, which I confess daily! This is my confession:

Father God, I thank You for the word of warning and the word of encouragement that You gave me in Deuteronomy 1. You said to me, "Cindy, don't be terrified; don't be afraid of recurring cancer. The Lord your God, who is going before you, will continue to fight for you, just as He did when He first healed your body of cancer before your very eyes. You saw how the Lord your God carried you, the way a father carries his child. He will continue to go ahead of you on your blessed journey." (Personal paraphrase of Deuteronomy 1:29-33.)

An important facet of the book of Deuteronomy is the "faith-plus-obedience" formula. Israel was called to trust God with their whole being and to obey His commands unswervingly. Faith plus obedience would enable them to inherit the promises with God's full blessing. The absence of faith and obedience, on the other hand, would introduce the cycle of failure and judgment. I want to inherit the promise of God's full blessing for my abundant life!

The next scripture of my spiritual warfare confession comes from Deuteronomy, chapter 28, verses 1 and 7 NIV: *If you fully obey the Lord your God and carefully follow all His commands I give you today . . . the Lord will grant that the enemies who rise up against you will be defeated before you. They will come at you from one direction, but they will flee from you in seven!*

My faith was strong and growing stronger by the day. And I was truly striving towards obedience to my God and His Word.

Remember, there is power in the Word, power to build up your faith, power to move mountains. The symptoms in my neck gradually disappeared. I had defeated cancer; I had defeated Satan!

So ends my healing testimony. I stand in awe of my almighty God and Father. He turned around the Stage 4 incurable cancer diagnosis with the prognosis of death into divine healing and abundant, complete life! I continuously pour out my thanksgiving and praise to God for every breath that I breathe and for every precious day of life!

But my story is far from ended …
my blessed journey continues!

# Part Two

# GOD IS NOT A RESPECTER OF PERSONS

*I* received my healing! Jesus paid the price for my healing. He provided it, and I received it. I often pray a prayer similar to this: "O mighty God, I give You all the glory and praise for my healing! Thank You for the wonderful gift of life. I embrace it as a priceless gift from You! And now I offer my life back to You. Use me, Father. I desire to serve You. Open a door, and expand my territory to serve You."

God has opened door after door after door after door in my life and has given me the opportunity to serve Him and His people through a healing ministry. What a joy, what an honor, what a privilege – but what a responsibility!

I started receiving phone calls and requests shortly after my healing. Most of them came from cancer patients or their loved ones. They all had one thing in common: They were all desperately seeking physical healing.

The most important theme that runs through each of the testimonies that I will share in this section of my book, is that <u>God is not a respecter of persons</u> (Acts 10:34). When Jesus was walking on this earth, He healed ALL who were sick. The truth of the Word is for ALL who believe. Jesus died for the redemption of ALL humanity, if they will only accept it!

As I started following the leading of the Holy Spirit and ministering to these people, I started seeing healings and changes of diagnoses left and right ... Terminal brain cancer is no longer cancer! A highly suspicious tumor with feelers into a heart is negative for cancer! Stage 4 lung cancer is in complete remission! Extremely suspicious blood counts are negative when tested for leukemia! An undiagnosed disease, with a suspicion of cancer, confusing doctors for months, is proven negative for cancer, is finally diagnosed, and completely cured! Stage 4 breast cancer is totally gone!

These are all healings I have been a witness to. I ministered to these real people facing real battles of life or death. The anointing of the Holy Spirit gave me the words as I shared my testimony. I shared God's promises regarding healing. I prayed in agreement with them. And they are all whole today and living an abundant life!

I am ecstatic and energized in my faith as I witness the power of God's healing. I am awestruck by the mightiness of our God. And I am truly humbled that He would use me as a minister of His Word and of His divine healing.

In this part of *A Blessed Journey*, I will share three incredible testimonies of healing. These three families have their loved ones with them today ... alive, whole, and healed by the power of God. *God is not a respecter of persons.* God heals today! Hallelujah!

## Chapter Sixteen

# THE BROCKBANK FAMILY

*K*arie Brockbank has been my very dear friend for many years. She walked with me through my battle with cancer, she witnessed the magnificent work of God in my life, and then she made the choice to surrender her own life to the Lord. That's how testimonies work … they bring hope to the hopeless, turn fear into faith, and lead the defeated into victory!

Karie had been afflicted with a virus in her vocal cords for about four years before I was diagnosed with cancer. The virus required multiple laser surgeries, which took place about every six months. Karie was devastated and consumed with fear with each new report that the virus was back. She believed that it was a condition she would have to learn to live with. Karie didn't know that she had a choice NOT to believe in the lifelong condition, but rather TO believe and receive God's precious healing!

Karie had a Bible and tried to read it, but she didn't understand much of what she read. *For the god of this world has blinded the unbelievers' minds [that they should not discern the truth], preventing them from seeing the illuminating light of the*

*Gospel of the glory of Christ (the Messiah), Who is the Image and Likeness of God* (2 Corinthians 4:4 AMP). She had even attended a huge nondenominational church and had been invited to pray the prayer of salvation, but she wasn't taught the biblical foundation of salvation in Jesus Christ and wasn't ready to take that step.

However, when Karie saw what God was doing in my life, she made the life-changing decision to pray the prayer of salvation. She started to learn and to grow in the ways of the Lord. When she realized that she did not have to live with the vocal cord condition, that she also could receive the precious healing of God, she started her journey of healing with what she calls "baby faith." She was not completely committed, but she was open to learn. As she confessed her healing, that by Jesus' stripes she too had been healed (1 Peter 2:24), the consuming fear that she had experienced with each new onset of the virus was extinguished!

She did have a few more surgeries after she began her faith walk, but with each surgery, the medical report improved, with the virus being less and less aggressive, and literally shrinking in size and strength. With each improved report, her faith grew stronger and stronger. The last surgery she had, which was three years ago, involved removing just a teeny tiny little smidge of the weak, defeated virus. Today Karie continues to stand firmly on God's Word that by the stripes of Jesus, her vocal cords have been totally, completely healed.

Throughout this season of Karie's life, Tom, her husband, had been quite skeptical of Karie's newfound faith. He frequently questioned and debated the absolute truth of the Word which Karie had been sharing with him. He was trying to process the Word of God intellectually—trying to make logical sense out of the salvation, redemption, and healing message. But as he witnessed my healing from Stage 4 melanoma, and his wife's improving medical report, he began to think that perhaps there was something to this whole idea that God heals today!

Then, just a few months after Karie started her faith journey, Tom was afflicted with a detached retina. The diagnosis came after symptoms of flashes in his eye, "floaters" in his vision, and finally blindness in the eye. He required immediate surgery to save his eyesight. He was warned that the surgery might not be 100 percent successful, that his vision might not be completely restored. He was also warned that the likelihood of having a detached retina in his other eye was very high.

Tom underwent the surgery. During the recovery process in the days following the surgery, Tom was depressed, unsure of his health and of the future of his eyesight. At that point, Karie asked Tom if he wanted to talk to me about God's healing, and he said "yes"!

The Lord had gone before me and totally prepared Tom to receive the truth into his heart. When I talked to him he was not defensive, or analytical, trying to reason out the "hows" and the "whys" of God's healing. I simply shared the foundational biblical truths of healing, through the anointing of the Holy Spirit, and Tom listened and believed. I prayed with Tom for the healing of his retina, and for the complete restoration of his vision.

When I stood up to leave, I was strongly prompted by the Holy Spirit that the message I had delivered was not complete, that I needed to ask Tom if he wanted to pray for his salvation. I sat right back down and said, "Tom, do you want to ask Jesus into your heart right now?" He immediately said, "Yes, I do!"

Karie and I prayed with Tom as he asked Jesus into his life, to be his Lord and Savior. Tom's physical circumstance involving his wounded eyesight had led him to a spiritual healing of his inward blindness, just like the Apostle Paul! (Acts 9). The light of Jesus was manifested in his heart! Hallelujah!

After asking Jesus into his life, Tom had a calmness and a peace about his physical well-being. And he didn't keep debating and questioning the Word of God. He opened his spiritual eyes to spiritual things. In the childhood of his life, his mother had shared profound words of wisdom with Tom. She always told him, "Tom, don't try to reason out the things of God. Just believe." Finally, he had taken his mother's excellent advice!

Within the next few weeks, Tom called me on two occasions when fear was trying to reattach itself to him. He had started having similar symptoms to the first detached retina. (This is a common ploy of the enemy.) I talked with him, supported him, coached him regarding standing strong on the Word, joined my faith with his, and we prayed the prayer of agreement. But Tom continued to have concerns with his vision. He went to the doctor, and had his eyes checked. When the doctor examined his eyes, he found the retina was completely healed! That's what we had prayed for, and that's what Tom received. Praise God! He has had no recurring vision concerns. He is whole and healed, physically and spiritually!

I have often seen faith energized as people see the power of God working in their lives. A few months later, when Tom and Karie's son, Brendan, faced a serious health concern, their faith went into overdrive and totally annihilated the enemy!

Tom and Karie took two-year-old Brendan to a golf range to hit a few golf balls. Within five minutes of arriving, Brendan picked up a mushroom and ate it. They immediately rushed him to the hospital. The emergency room doctor gave Brendan ipecac to induce vomiting, and then sent Tom back to the golf course to bring them a sample of the mushroom that Brendan had eaten. They soon determined that it was a deathly poisonous mushroom called "Fallen Angel." (Satan is very clever, isn't he?)

At that point, they did a battery of tests on Brendan's liver, which is where this particular poisonous mushroom typically attacks the body. Although the mushroom did not affect him (he probably had not actually swallowed it), the test showed that the balance of enzymes in his liver was alarmingly off.

Within the next couple of days, he was retested, and with each retest, the enzyme level came back even higher. Brendan's pediatrician referred him to the chief of hemotology at Children's Hospital to do a bone scan. What Karie and Tom didn't know at that time was that the doctors were suspicious of leukemia.

At this point, Karie and Tom's faith went into overdrive. Karie is a woman who typically worries excessively over insignificant concerns. But in this instance, with the intense power of a praying mom, she assertively took authority over Brendan's health. She poured herself into the Word. She confessed the scripture, "By Jesus' stripes Brendan has been healed" constantly and fervently. She discovered that the more she filled herself with the Word of God and confessed the healing scripture, the more her mind was protected from negative thoughts and worry. She did NOT lose control to fear and worry. She did not focus on the circumstance, she focused on the solution! She leaned on me as her support system in faith, and I prayed with her in agreement for Brendan's health.

Karie stood firm and strong—until she actually walked into Children's Hospital with Tom and Brendan. The office where they were directed had the name, "Pediatric Oncology" on the window. That is when Karie momentarily lost control. I was at work that day, and when I received her frantic phone call, God enabled me to minister to her right then and there, praying a fervent prayer of agreement with her. She calmed down, and walked into the Pediatric Oncology Unit. She did not allow fear to consume her when she saw all the precious children obviously battling cancer. Rather, she focused on God's promise of healing and went in with her son and her husband to meet the specialist.

The chief of hemotology examined Brendan's muscles and joints carefully, and asked many questions regarding his energy level, his appetite, and his general health. Then, to their surprise, he told Karie and Tom that he did not feel it was necessary to do a bone scan. He took another blood test, and the enzyme level was still far out of balance. However, when he conferred with other specialists they agreed that Brendan's enzyme level was simply an anomaly and normal for Brendan. At this point, Karie and Tom were outwardly praising God!

Karie later told me that when she prayed the healing scripture over Brendan, she believed that God was surrounding Brendan with an armor of protection. Her faith grew. Tom's faith grew. For the first time in their lives, they had revelation understanding of the power of prayer.

Today this little family is whole and healthy and seeking to continue to grow up spiritually! And they continue to praise God for His awesome love and the healing they have received from Him!

## Chapter Seventeen

# GARY HALLS

*N*ancy Halls teaches in the school where I am a Learning Consultant. I started a Teachers in Touch prayer group to bring prayer into our school about six months after I had received my healing from cancer. We pray for the students, their families, the teachers, and our own personal needs. Nancy joined our group in January of 2003 after a close family friend had been killed in a plane crash, leaving behind a young wife and children. She simply wanted to pray for this family as they struggled through their mourning process. Little did she know how desperately she would need the power of prayer in her own life very soon.

Gary, Nancy's husband of twenty-eight years, awoke one morning to discover a large lump on his arm. He had been sleeping with his arm outstretched, his head on his arm. He noticed an egg-size lump on the interior side of his arm, right above the elbow joint. He showed Nancy, and she immediately thought he should have it checked. But he didn't follow her advice.

Gary had been an avid baseball player as a kid and a young man. He had even played professionally for a couple of years. He was a pitcher and had suffered related injuries. Gary also exercised avidly, and thought perhaps he had torn a muscle during his workout, although he didn't have any pain. He related the lump in his arm to past or recent sports injuries, and didn't even let it concern him.

But Nancy was very concerned. She came to me right away for support. We talked; we prayed. I gave Nancy the Charles Capps booklet, *Creative Power for Healing*. Gary and Nancy began declaring the healing scriptures together and listening to healing scriptures on tape. They also began to read the Bible and pray together.

About two weeks after his initial discovery of the lump, Gary finally showed it to Tim, a colleague from work. Tim works out with Gary, is a close friend and a believer. Tim told Gary that he needed to call a doctor right away. Then Tim went home to his wife Ann, and they began praying for Gary.

That same evening, Gary finally did make an appointment with a doctor. The doctor carefully examined his arm, and said he believed Gary had a distal rupture of his bicep. Gary was confused. It simply didn't make sense, since he had absolutely no pain. The doctor referred him to an orthopedic surgeon, whom he saw two days later.

Orthopedic surgeons frequently treat sports injuries. As this doctor examined Gary's arm, Gary told him of his history as a professional pitcher, and the injuries he had sustained as a result. The doctor, so intent upon his examination, never even looked up or acknowledged Gary's sports history. Instead, he told him, "Your bicep is fine, Gary. But there's a mass in there." He scheduled him for an MRI at 8:00 a.m. the following morning.

Gary had the MRI. After the results were reviewed, Gary was referred to an oncologist.

The oncologist specialized in sarcoma. She looked at the 380 frames of MRI film and said that if she had to bet, she'd say that Gary had sarcoma. She reported the path that sarcoma usually takes; that the cancer travels through the bloodstream, usually attacking the lungs, and then other organs.

Even with this report, Gary simply couldn't believe it! He had no pain (but pain never accompanies the initial onset of sarcoma). He felt strong. He was not in fear. He simply wanted to take care of this problem and go on with his life! But Nancy, his wife, was a world class worrier. I've known Nancy for about ten years. I've seen her worry extensively over many minor situations. But in this life-threatening situation, I saw a Nancy I'd never seen before! She had a calmness and a peace about her that was beyond the natural! Just as Jesus calmed the winds and the waves in the storm at sea, I believe He calmed the storm in her family's lives. They were strong and confident that their prayers would absolutely be answered!

Soft tissue sarcomas are malignant tumors that can develop from fat, muscle, nerve, fibrous tissues surrounding joints, blood vessels, or deep skin tissues. They can develop in any part of the body. About half of them develop in the arms or legs. In 2005, about 9,420 new soft tissue sarcomas were diagnosed in the United States, and about 3,490 Americans died of the disease.[1]

---

[1]www.cancer.org/docroot/CRI/content/CRI_2_4_1X_What_is_sarcoma_38.asp?site area= and www.cancer.org/docroot/ CRI_2_4_1X_What_are_the_ key_statistics_for sarcoma _38.asp?may_cri, accessed September 2005.

The tumor in Gary's arm was 6.5 cm x 6 cm x 3.5 cm. If it were proven to be positive for cancer, it would be considered high grade; Stage 3, with a 56 percent five-year survival rate. The surgery to remove the tumor was scheduled five days after his appointment with the oncologist.

Gary made a trip to Chicago during this waiting period. His mother had passed away about three months prior, and he was helping to take care of affairs in regards to her death. As he was driving that night, he thought he felt the tumor getting bigger, and his arm was swelling. He began to panic and called Nancy. She helped her husband through that fear, supporting him, comforting him, and agreeing with him for his wholeness and healing.

The Halls family drew close together in prayer as they agreed for Gary's healing. Nancy and Gary continued to declare healing scriptures over Gary's body and to read the Bible together. Joanna, their youngest daughter, requested prayer from all the children in her Christian youth group, praying in unity for her father. Jennifer, Gary and Nancy's oldest daughter, is a very fervent Christian. She meets with a small group weekly at her minister's house for Bible study, prayer, and fellowship. The night before Gary's surgery, he went with Jennifer to her Bible study. The minister laid hands on Gary and prayed for his healing.

Jennifer had also been praying for a Christian doctor. The next day, when the surgeon came in to go over procedures before the surgery, Jennifer noticed that she was wearing a cross, and boldly asked her if she was a Christian, to which she responded, "Yes!" Gary, Nancy, Jennifer, Julie (their middle daughter), and the surgeon all prayed in unity to our awesome God before Gary went into surgery.

Then Nancy waited. Hours later, the surgeon came out to see Nancy. She knelt in front of her, and with a heart of compassion said, "I'm sorry, Nancy. The tumor was high-grade sarcoma."

Nancy called me that day. I was in Seattle, taking care of my own son who had had a skiing injury which required surgery. I remember her calm demeanor. I encouraged her with the truth of the Word. We prayed once again in agreement that Gary would receive the healing Jesus had already provided for him and that it would be totally manifested in his body.

In a cancer surgery, they typically do an initial frozen biopsy of the tumor right in surgery. If the biopsy is positive, it confirms the existence of cancer immediately, which was the case with Gary. However, even if it is negative, it is still possible that there are cancer cells in the tumor. Therefore, the suspect tissue must be thoroughly tested by pathology. This report came back two days later and confirmed the initial diagnosis, positive for sarcoma. However, the result of this pathology report was slightly different than the initial frozen biopsy, now staging the sarcoma as low grade.

Gary remained in the hospital for additional testing. The scans of his other organs came back clear. Then the doctor sent him home to heal from the surgery. The plan was to begin radiation treatments in four weeks.

Gary had an excellent doctor, guided with wisdom from above! Since the staging in the two biopsy reports was conflicting, she made the decision to send the tissue on to Boston Medical Center for further testing. Two-and-a-half weeks later, Gary got an incredible phone call from his doctor. She said that there had been a mistake; the tumor was NOT cancerous after all! It was totally benign! Gary didn't have sarcoma; he had nodular fasciitis, a benign tumor commonly misdiagnosed as sarcoma. No further treatment was necessary! How could the same tumor possibly go from high-grade sarcoma, to low-grade sarcoma, to benign nodular facsiitis? With our mighty God, anything is possible!

Now, Gary is whole and healthy. He and Nancy continue to grow spiritually as they study God's Word in small group settings. They go to church faithfully. They discuss God's work in their lives and in the lives of their three beautiful daughters, Jennifer, Julie, and Joanna. They pray together.

Julie, Gary and Nancy's middle daughter, recently got married. In the months before the wedding, Gary spent quality time reading the Bible with Julie as she prepared to get married and join her life with her husband and with God. As the family prepared for the wedding, they counted their many blessings, and they gave God the glory for Gary's healing. Gary walked his daughter down the aisle, and he presented her to God and to her husband, rejoicing!

## Chapter Eighteen

# BEN HAYES

Karen and Ben met, fell in love, and got married in 1998. Ben had never known what love was until he loved Karen. He did not have a love-filled childhood. His parents had a rocky marriage ending in divorce, for which Ben irrationally blamed himself. He had a broken relationship with his sister, which greatly troubled him. And he had a dream when he was very young that he would die before he was thirty years old. He had openly shared this dream with others since childhood, and was adamant that it would come to pass. There is power in the spoken word, and Ben literally spoke the negative into existence.

Ben's battle for his life started in February of 2003. He was having pain in his back, so he went to a chiropractor for an alignment. The chiropractor x-rayed him and saw scar tissue in his lungs that was very abnormal for a twenty-eight-year-old man. He went to his primary care doctor, who gave him a PFT (pulmonary function test), the results of which were absolutely normal. Ben requested a CT scan, which showed scarring in his lungs. Ben was referred to a pulmonary specialist.

The doctor ordered a biopsy of Ben's lungs, which revealed lesions consistent with sarcoid. These lesions cause damage to the lung tissue that heals by scarring. The doctor assured Ben that they were not unusual and that they would clear themselves up and go away. He prescribed large doses of steroids and sent him off to heal.

But Ben didn't heal. The large dosages of steroids were not helping the sarcoidosis in the least, and they were causing severe side effects in Ben's disposition. By November of 2003, Ben's lungs were much worse, and he was coughing up blood. He was given another PFT, which again came back normal. What the doctor had not discovered at this point is that even though he could breath air normally, his lungs were not exchanging oxygen efficiently. Ben was frustrated with his doctor, but since he was in a HMO insurance group, he didn't have access to the pulmonary specialists at the University of Michigan Medical Center whom he desperately needed to see.

By June 2004, Ben had lost thirty pounds and was gravely ill. He had great difficulty breathing. Ben finally decided, with or without insurance coverage, he needed to get a second opinion from the University of Michigan Medical Center. He was frequently coughing up blood. He couldn't keep any food down. After a trip to the emergency room on July 26, he was admitted to the University of Michigan Medical Center and began eight days of extensive testing.

That testing finally revealed the true condition of Ben's lungs. One of his lungs was only exchanging oxygen at a 20 percent capacity, and the other lung was totally blocked, completely filled with blood clots. The medical team was also gravely concerned about a blood clot which a CT scan had located centimeters from the aortic center of his heart. The doctors gave him oxygen to help him to breathe, instructed him to do absolutely nothing but sit, due to his grave heart concern, and continue his prescription of blood thinners to attempt to reduce the blood clotting in his lungs and in his heart. He was released from the hospital on August 3, only to be readmitted to intensive care on August 9, literally drowning in the blood in his lungs.

The University of Michigan transplant team evaluated Ben's test results. Another roadblock was hit when the transplant team determined that Ben was not a candidate for a transplant because he was only thirty years old and sarcoid is not considered chronic or irreversible. However, Ben's doctor knew Ben needed new lungs in order to live so he began searching for alternative treatments and transplant centers.

Ben's brother Ken is a strong believer. He came to see Ben in that intensive care unit. He brought Ben a Bible and told him about Jesus. Ben asked his brother if he was being punished for not being the person that God wanted him to be. Ken assured Ben that God is a wonderful, loving God and that the disease in his lungs was NOT punishment from God. It was not God's plan for Ben to die young. Ken led his brother in the prayer of salvation on August 11, 2004. Ben instantly felt as though a heavy weight had been lifted off of him. He was completely and totally spiritually healed, praise God!

Ben was taken off the blood thinners. He gradually coughed up less and less blood, and was released from the hospital on August 12. On August 18, a procedure to stint open a vein in Ben's lungs was unsuccessful.

After Ben accepted Jesus, he started praying and ravenously feeding on God's Word in the Holy Bible. He had tons of questions and would seek answers from Karen, his brother Ken, or Ken's wife, Melissa. Throughout the remainder of his battle, he depended upon God's Word and prayer to keep him strong, and to calm him during times of fear or depression. *For when I am weak [in human strength], then am I [truly] strong (able, powerful in divine strength)* (2 Corinthians 12:10 AMP).

God's blessed favor began to flow into Karen and Ben's lives. After ongoing, overwhelming problems with their current insurance, Karen finally discovered that there was a no-predisposition clause which enabled her to leave her HMO insurance and change to an insurance that did not limit them to use only in-network physicians. This insurance change required a 120-day waiting period. Their insurance changed over on October 10, 2004, and Ben had his first appointment with the transplant specialist, Dr. Budev, at the Cleveland Clinic on October 11. Karen had done her homework, and had all Ben's tests on disc and all of his medical records and reports gathered.

In Ohio, a patient has to be approved by the hospital transplant team to have their case taken to the Ohio Consortium. The Ohio Consortium then makes the decision whether or not the transplant is ethical. There was much discussion on whether Ben should get one lung, two lungs, or a heart/lung combination. After much discussion, Ben was approved for a double lung transplant.

Kent and I met Ben in November of 2004. My niece and Ben's wife, Karen, are best friends. My brother and sister told Kent and me about Ben and his lung trauma one Friday night as we chatted over dinner. That night and the next morning I was very burdened to intercede for Ben, both in prayer and in action. I contacted my niece to get Karen and Ben's phone number and I called. Karen knew about my healing of cancer, and was very anxious to talk to me. Kent and I planned a visit for the very next day.

Kent and I have been blessed to minister to many people in need of healing, but never before had the Holy Spirit anointed our ministry so powerfully. When Kent and I walked into Ben and Karen's house, we saw a man in a chair, hooked up to oxygen and covered with a blanket. Ben's physical body was a frail shell of a man, but his spirit man was alive and hungry for knowledge and truth. He and Karen were so open to receive all that God had for them, and Kent and I were the vessels He used to deliver to them the truth that Jesus had already paid the price for Ben's healing, and that it was NOT God's plan for Ben to die, but to live and to declare the works of the Lord!

We shared the truth that there is power in God's spoken Word; power to build yourself up in faith, and power to receive the healing already paid for by our Savior, Jesus Christ. We also talked about the power in the negative spoken word, and warned Ben to never speak death over his body again by repeating the statement that he believed he would die before he was thirty years old. (Jesus said that we would get what we believe! See Mark 11:22-24.)

I was working on this very book at that time and assured Ben that his healing would be a chapter in it. I gave him a draft copy of this unfinished book, and I gave him Charles Capps' booklet with healing confessions, *Creative Power for Healing*. I laid hands on Ben, and we prayed together in agreement believing in absolute faith that the healing that Jesus suffered and died for would be manifest in Ben's body!

That same evening after we left, Karen helped Ben take a shower. Ben stood in the shower, struggling just to hold himself up, while his wife washed his back with loving hands, and Ben asked Karen, "Should we wait for a miracle instead of going ahead with a lung transplant?"

Karen answered, "Ben, if we get your new lungs, that IS our miracle!"

Ben started diligently and fervently confessing the healing scriptures over his body, especially his lungs and his heart. I called Karen the next day, concerned that Ben did not have enough lung capacity to say the prayers aloud, so I suggested they audio tape Ben saying the confessions so he could just listen to them. She told me, "Aunt Cindy, it's amazing. He starts out very weak, but the more he prays, the stronger his voice becomes. He can say the prayers!" But she had him tape them anyway, which was to be valuable beyond imagination very soon.

Karen also began confessing healing scriptures over her husband daily. She frequently laid hands on him as she prayed the scriptures. Together, their faith grew stronger and stronger.

Two weeks to the day after our visit, Ben's lungs began to shut down. He was alternately lying on the couch, then sitting up, trying to get in a position where he could get enough oxygen to breathe. He told Karen, "I can't lie back down, or I'm afraid I will never get up again." He agreed to go to the hospital, but it was all Karen could do to help him get into the car to drive him to the University of Michigan Medical Center. The only things they took with them were Ben's Bible, his prayers, and his tape player with the recorded confessions.

When he arrived, his fingernails and lips were blue, the doctors could not even gather a pulse ox from the fingertip device, and his resting heart rate was 163 beats per minute. Ben was admitted immediately and given a private room. The doctors thought at first that he was suffering from pneumonia, but that was not the case. He needed a lung transplant and he needed it soon. The doctors did what they could to sustain Ben with antibiotics, muscle relaxants, IV liquids, and of course oxygen. Throughout this harrowing week, Ben fed upon God's Word to keep him calm, to sustain him with the spiritual food that he needed even more desperately than he needed oxygen.

Karen talked to the transplant specialist, Dr. Budev, on Tuesday. She warned Karen of the immense risk involved in the transplant surgery, especially given as desperately sick as Ben was. Karen replied, "Dr. Budev, the way I see it, there are three possible outcomes. If we do nothing, my husband will die. If we do the transplant, my husband may die. Or if we do the transplant, my husband may live. I believe with all my heart that my husband **will live**!" Dr. Budev received permission to add Ben to the lung transplant list on Friday at 10:00 a.m.

But that date was moved up to Wednesday through the favor of God. Now remember Karen's earlier statement that getting a pair of lungs would be God's miracle for Ben? Dr. Budev had told Karen and Ben that the soonest she had ever gotten lungs for a transplant patient was seven days. But Ben's new lungs were received just thirty hours after he was placed on the transplant list, right in the city of Cleveland!

Karen got a phone call on Thursday morning at 10:00 a.m. that lungs were available, and that they were a possible match. At 4:00 in the afternoon they got the word that the match was perfect. At that point, Ben's family gathered together for prayer. Ken, Ben's mother, his younger sister, and Karen all gathered around Ben. Ken prayed, "Father God, You are so immense! We know that You created heaven and earth in seven days. This lung transplant is small for You, and we <u>know</u> that You can do this for Ben! We release Ben into Your loving hands."

After the extended family left to drive to Cleveland, Ben and Karen waited for the air transport to arrive. And in this quiet moment, Ben told Karen that God had spoken to him the night before. He told Ben, "Buddy, everything's going to be fine." Karen was positive and full of faith, but also very nervous about the upcoming transplant surgery. Ben, on the other hand, was perfectly calm.

Ben traveled wonderfully. His stats were stable and he was holding his own. But as soon as he was settled into the Intensive Care Unit at the Cleveland Clinic, his stats suddenly started to drop at an alarming rate. Ben was going into respiratory arrest. God's timing is so incredibly perfect. His new lungs were waiting for him. The transplant team was gathered. Now his exhausted lungs could finally rest. Ben looked at Karen and said, "I love you and I'll see you in the morning." They inserted a ventilator, and prepared him for surgery.

Dr. Budev was there as well. She told Karen, "We're making medical history tonight. The only reason our team has agreed to do this surgery is because of the love you have for one another and because of your faith."

The surgeons began their work at 2:00 a.m. The team told Karen that the surgery would last for eight to twelve hours. During the night, Karen dozed, waking every hour to turn Ben's prayer tape on, and then would doze again to the sound of her husband's voice speaking God's Word on healing. Now Ben's prayers were bringing Karen a peace that was beyond all understanding! The surgery was completed at 7:30 a.m., only five-and-a-half hours from start to finish! The surgery was completely successful. The lungs were a perfect fit. And they had literally taken Ben's heart out of his chest cavity, examined it, and it was absolutely perfect! The blood clot indicated by the CT scan did not exist!

Ben was on the ventilator for several days. At times when he was anxious, he would hold his hands in a praying position, and Karen would ask, "Ben, do you want to hear your prayers?" He would nod "yes." Karen played his healing confession tape over and over. He would calm down, his heart rate would slow, and he would rest peacefully.

Ben's vocal cords were paralyzed due to an injury caused by the ventilator. But when it was finally removed, he whispered the following statement, "It's a beautiful day, God is good, and I love my wife with all my heart!" Karen cried with thanksgiving!

Ben had a few more obstacles to overcome in his victory over death. The doctors told him it would take up to a year for his vocal cords to heal, but that they could do surgery to repair them. Ben said, "No way!" and proceeded to believe God for his voice to return. His voice was completely restored within one month!

When Ben could again begin to eat, he weighed only 142 pounds. But he couldn't keep down any food. The doctors began another round of tests to determine the cause of this complication. They were concerned that perhaps a blood vessel had gotten twisted or improperly placed during surgery or that he had an intestinal blockage. But Karen and Ben wouldn't receive those problems. Karen laid hands on Ben and confessed that Ben was whole from the top of his head to the bottom of his feet, with nothing missing and nothing broken.

With a scoping of Ben's stomach, they discovered a large ulcer the size of his thumbnail, which was the culprit of his inability to hold food down. A simple medicine stopped that problem ... and Ben could eat again! (He now weighs a healthy 182 pounds!)

The transplant team had initially told Ben and Karen that he would be in Cleveland for eight weeks, but he went home after only four-and-a-half weeks! Those days of recovery were long and difficult. Encouragement came through the support and love of his wife, his family, his friends, and his heavenly Father. Ben constantly read the Bible during times of frustration or depression. *Remain in me, and I will remain in you* (John 15:4 NIV). *Come near to God and he will come near to you* (James 4:8 NIV). The Father was with Ben, carrying him as a father carries his child!

Karen and Ben made friends with several other transplant patients. They witnessed successful transplants and they witnessed failed attempts at this life-giving surgery. They realized that those with faith in God received their healing lungs, and those without faith rejected the lungs and life.

Ben is a new man. When I interviewed him for his testimony for his chapter of my book, he was smiling, strong, and full of life. But like me, Ben has received so much more than just his physical healing. In his old life, Ben was not a kind man. He did not live a life of love. Before he got sick, he was driven to work hard in order to gain material things. He put his job and material things before everything, even his wife. He had no desire to give of himself to anyone for any reason. But now Ben is a new man on the inside. He seeks God first in his life. He loves his wife and treats her like gold. He does not have a heart of stone. He has a heart of flesh! As we talked, he laughed and cried and openly expressed his love for his wife and for his heavenly Father.

Ben's vision has changed. He no longer sees himself a dead man. He sees himself as a living, breathing vessel of God, ready to do His will!

# *Part Three*

# GOD'S ITINERARY

*W*hen I was first diagnosed with cancer, the intellectual part of me knew that I needed knowledge and information regarding cancer and treatments. I needed to research, read, study, learn, and carefully weigh my options regarding crucial life or death decisions.

But in the spiritual realm, natural intellect doesn't always apply. We must seek godly wisdom regarding health. In fact, the Word even urges us to pray for wisdom in James 1:5: *If any of you lacks wisdom, let him ask of God, who gives to all liberally and without reproach, and it will be given to him.* I never disregarded the doctors' reports or their suggestions. But the truth of the Word takes precedence over the facts in the natural. I chose to believe God's report over the doctor's report. I focused my energies and my research on one resource, God's living Word, the Bible.

Part 3 of this book can lead you on the same journey that I took, with the same results that I got. Chapter 19, "The Great Exchange," and chapter 20, "Healing Is Conditional," teach rich, fundamental truths regarding healing as given to us through God's Word. Take time to savor them, read and reread them, focusing particularly on the scriptures that support these truths. Total belief in these truths is critical to receiving your healing.

Don't try to figure them out intellectually. Faith is believing what you don't see, what you may not understand intellectually.

The remainder of *A Blessed Journey* lays out God's itinerary for you to receive your own healing and so much more! Each step is crucial; leave none of them out. Your entire life <u>will</u> be transformed, <u>if</u> you follow God's plan. When I started my journey, I was simply desperate to hang on to my physical life, but I got so much more than I was seeking! God *is able to do exceedingly abundantly above all that we ask or think, according to the power that works in us* (Ephesians 3:20). God's plan is that we live an abundant life and enjoy eternal life in the fellowship of our Father ... beginning today!

## Chapter Nineteen

# THE GREAT EXCHANGE

The Bible gives us an excellent explanation of "The Great Exchange" in Romans, chapter 5, verses 12-21. I would suggest that you study this chapter carefully, reading it in several translations, especially in the more contemporary versions such as *The New International Version* (NIV), the *New Living Translation* (NLT), or the *Message Bible*. Allow these scriptures to feed you, to reveal to you what a magnificent gift Jesus provided for you! The Apostle Paul teaches us that "The Great Exchange" involved two distinct people, Adam and Jesus.

First, we need to look back at God's original plan, in the days of Adam and Eve. God created man to fellowship with Him, to love, to praise, and to worship Him. He gave man dominion, or authority, over the world. *Then God said, "Let Us make man in Our image, according to Our likeness; let them have dominion over the fish of the sea, over the birds of the air, and over the cattle, over all the earth and over every creeping thing that creeps on the earth"* . . . *Then God blessed them, and God said to them, "Be fruitful and multiply; fill the earth and subdue it . . ."* (Genesis 1:26,28).

Adam and Eve were blessed and living in unbroken fellowship with God. They had never known sickness, pain, grief, or poverty. But when Adam and Eve gave in to the temptation of Satan, they lost everything that God had blessed them with! Their fellowship with God was broken, and in its place was eternal damnation. With Adam's sin came the fall of man. Through this one man, sin entered the world. Sin opened the door to sickness, disease, poverty, fear, depression, worry, and all that is evil in the world.

The ultimate penalty of sin was spiritual death (separation from God) and physical death. At the fall of man, Adam gave his authority over to Satan, and humanity received the sin nature, together with all of its negative effects.

But beginning in Romans, chapter 5, verse 15, the Bible tells us that Jesus' rescuing gift is not exactly parallel to Adam's death-dealing sin. When Jesus died, He destroyed spiritual death. And He destroyed sin and the effects of sin, including sickness and pain! EVERYTHING that was lost to us through the curse of Adam's original sin was destroyed! Not one thing that was lost through Adam and Eve's falling was left standing! What God accomplished through His Son's death and resurrection far surpasses what Satan accomplished through the fall of Adam and Eve.

Romans 5:15 AMP says: *But God's free gift is not at all to be compared to the trespass [His grace is out of all proportion to the fall of man]. For if many died through one man's falling away (his lapse, his offense), much more profusely did God's grace and the free gift [that comes] through the undeserved favor of the one Man Jesus Christ abound and overflow to and for [the benefit of] many.*

Jesus, our Savior, paid the price for our sin, and made a public spectacle of Satan, destroying his power, and giving authority over sin and its effects to the believer!

Just read this awesome scripture, Colossians 2:14-15 in the Amplified Translation! *Having cancelled and blotted out and wiped away the handwriting of the note (bond) with its legal decrees and demands which was in force and stood against us (hostile to us). This [note with its regulations, decrees, and demands] He set aside and cleared completely out of our way by nailing it to [His] cross. [God] disarmed the principalities and powers that were ranged against us and made a bold display and public example of them, in triumphing over them in Him and in it [the cross].*

Romans 4:25 AMP is also wonderful: [Jesus], *who was betrayed and put to death because of our misdeeds and was raised to secure our justification (our acquittal), [making our account balance and absolving us from all guilt before God].*

These scriptures say that Jesus disarmed Satan and his demons, triumphing over them through His death and resurrection! They say that He blotted out the legal decree that stood against us, while Satan had dominion over this earth. They say that we were acquitted, found not guilty, and our accounts were balanced, paid in full! Even though we deserved the penalty of spiritual death because of our sin, Jesus paid off our debt and balanced our account for us! But it is up to us to receive this gift from God!

Let's continue with the analogy of the bank account. You may have millions of dollars in the bank, but if you don't access your funds, you could literally die of starvation! In the same way, you can die an eternal death, separated from God forever, without receiving the gift of forgiveness and salvation from your Father. And you can suffer with pain and sickness, and even die an early death, because you didn't accept and receive the healing gift that Jesus has already provided for you.

We, as believers, have authority over sin, sickness, pain, poverty, fear, depression, worry, and all the evils of human life. *[The Father] has delivered and drawn us to Himself out of the control and the dominion of darkness and has transferred us into the kingdom of the Son of His love, in whom we have our redemption through His blood, [which means] the forgiveness of our sins* (Colossians 1:13-14 AMP).

I didn't know this fundamental truth as I grew up! I didn't know that the Father had delivered me and drawn me to Himself, out of the control of Satan, and had transferred me into the kingdom of Jesus, through the redemption of Jesus' precious blood! I knew that Jesus had died for my sins and to give me eternal life, but I didn't know about all that other great stuff! But now I do know!

According to God's Word, the life-giving gift of Jesus is <u>better</u> than the death-dealing sin of Adam. And if Adam's sin ushered in sin, sickness, pain, poverty, spiritual and physical death, then Jesus' gift wiped all of that out. He paid the price for our healing; *by his wounds you have been healed* (1 Peter 2:24 NIV)! It's already been done, once and for all!

Satan has blinded humanity with half-truths regarding Jesus' gift. But I believe the <u>whole truth</u> of the redemptive power of Jesus' death and resurrection with every fiber of my being! Jesus died for my healing. I said "yes" to God with all of my heart and soul and strength, and I received the healing that Jesus had already provided for me. My friend, Jesus died for you every bit as much as He died for me. But it's up to you to say "yes" to Jesus and to receive His precious gift.

I saw the movie, "The Passion of Christ," as did millions and millions of people across the world. And I forced myself to keep my eyes open and watch how my Savior suffered for me. With each lash of the whip, with each stripe cut into His back, with each drop of blood that He shed for me, I declared, "By Your stripes, my Lord, I have been healed of cancer." Our Savior did not suffer and die in vain. He did His part, as amazing as it is that He would die for us while we were still sinners. It is up to us to do our part, to simply believe and to receive His precious gift of life ... spiritual life, physical life, and eternal life.

*Chapter Twenty*

# HEALING IS CONDITIONAL

This is a tough chapter with tough questions and even tougher answers. But the truth of God's Word will set you free ... free to be healed and to walk in divine health all the days of your life!

> **IF GOD IS GOOD, WHY THEN IS THERE SO MUCH SUFFERING AND PAIN AND MISERY IN OUR WORLD?**

God IS good and just and kind and merciful and forgiving. God is **not** the author of suffering and pain and misery. **Satan is.** Satan is the god of the world. Even though Jesus died to disarm the powers and principalities and to pay the price for our redemption, we still have a free will, and it is up to us to exercise our authority over evil.

**God's perfect will** is anything that God expressly desires for us. We know that the Word of God is the perfect will of God. For example, we know that He desires that everyone be saved (1 Timothy 2:4; 2 Peter 3:9). However, God's perfect will does not mean that His desire will automatically come to pass, because even though it is His desire, He has given us a free will to make our own choices.

**God's permissive will** refers to what God permits or allows to happen, even though He does not specifically desire it to happen. Much of what happens in this world is contrary to God's perfect will, yet He permits evil to continue for the time being. God does not <u>cause</u> sickness, but He does <u>allow</u> it.

## Causes of Sickness and Disease

So sickness and pain and suffering and misery are from Satan, but why does he choose one person over another to inflict his wrath upon? That's where we come in; we open the door and allow Satan into our lives. There are four general causes of sickness and disease.

1.  The first one goes back to <u>the fall of man</u>. When Adam gave his authority over to Satan, sin entered the world, which opened the door to sickness and disease upon mankind.

2.  The second cause for sickness and disease is <u>disobedience to the Word of God, or sin</u>. Sin may be **not doing** the things God told you to do; i.e., not being loving, not being patient or kind. Or sin can be **doing** the things that God explicitly tells you not to do, such as breaking the Ten Commandments. Sin opens the door to Satan's destruction in our lives. In my case, I now realize that I had a door wide open for Satan to attack me, due to the sin in my life.

    ❖ I had other idols before me. I did not put God first in my life. My career, my family, and even material things came before God in my life.

❖ I did not do what God tells us to do in His Word. I did not live a holy life, consecrated unto the Lord. I did not walk in love toward my neighbors with patience and kindness and goodness.

❖ I had unforgiveness and bitterness in my heart, which prevented God from forgiving my sins.

3. The third cause of sickness and disease is the <u>oppression of the devil</u>. Satan is the author of sickness and disease. *The thief comes only to steal and kill and destroy . . .* (John 10:10 NIV). Sickness can shorten our life span or lessen the quality of life that God intended for us to enjoy. It can cause men to question God's goodness. It can weaken our testimony so we cannot work to build up God's Kingdom.

4. The fourth cause of sickness and disease is <u>the law of sowing and reaping</u>. We will reap the seed that we are sowing. Just as a farmer reaps a corn crop when he plants a corn seed, we can reap sickness if we sow seeds (words) of that disease. In my case, since I loved to spend time in the sun, I often said things like: "I know that the sun isn't good for me, 'cause it can cause skin cancer." "I need to get a skin check. With all the sun I get I have to watch for skin cancer." "I know tanning booths aren't good for me, they can cause skin cancer," etc.

You see, **I** made the choice, albeit unknowingly, to allow Satan to inflict sickness upon me. The cancer I was diagnosed with could very easily have shortened my life span and lessoned the quality of life that God had intended for me to enjoy. And of course, God would not have been glorified. In fact, He may have even received the blame for my early death.

Let me reiterate that in all four causes of sickness and disease, WE are the ones who open the door to Satan and let him right in. It has nothing to do with God. But God must permit it, because He has given us a free will. It is NOT His perfect will for His people to be sick. He loves us. God IS love. And God in His infinite love does not desire sickness in His people. This is just one of many scriptures that shows how much we are loved by God: *Are not five sparrows sold for two pennies? Yet not one of them is forgotten by God. Indeed, the very hairs of your head are all numbered. Don't be afraid; you are worth more than many sparrows* (Luke 12:6-7 NIV).

Even though I KNOW that it is not God's will for His people to be sick or in pain, I also know that He can and does use desperate situations in our lives to strengthen us, to help us to grow, to develop our character, and to draw us closer to Him. *And we know that all things work together for good to those who love God, to those who are the called according to His purpose* (Romans 8:28). This scripture has come to pass in my life. Not only am I alive and completely healthy; I am living an abundant life, filled with the blessings of my almighty God! I have thanked God for doing a work in me while teaching me "how" to overcome cancer. When I had nowhere else to turn, I said "yes" to Jesus and to this amazing life that He paid the price for me to enjoy! The quality of my life after cancer is far above the quality of my life before cancer.

---

**WHY DO BAD THINGS HAPPEN TO GOOD PEOPLE? WHY ARE SOME PEOPLE HEALED, BUT NOT OTHERS?**

---

The rest of this book will be devoted to answering these two questions. But let me tell you what the answer to these questions is NOT. It is NOT God's will for some people to be healed and not others. Sickness is NOT God's method of chastisement, meant to train, to educate, or to teach us a lesson. And sickness does NOT bring glory to God in any way or form. Healing **is** conditional, but it is **not** conditional on whether or not it is God's will to heal us. Rather, it's conditional on whether or not **we do our part** to receive the healing Jesus has already provided for us through His death and resurrection!

Following is a "preview" and a "review"... A preview of God's itinerary for your journey to healing, and a review of the steps that I took to receive my healing.

- ✝ Give your life totally to God. Surrender to Him. Open up your heart and invite Him in as your Lord and Savior.
- ✝ Ask your Father for the baptism of the Holy Spirit, with power from on high. Then use your gift of tongues to pray the perfect will of God.
- ✝ Develop a relationship with your heavenly Father through a daily prayer life and fellowship with Abba Father, through daily reading and studying of His Word, through daily prayer in your understanding

and in tongues, and through sincere praise and worship of our mighty God!

✞ Have a sincere, absolute faith, or belief that you **are** the healed of the Lord! Build your faith through confessing the Word of God, consistently and frequently! This takes time!

✞ Be IN the will of God. Obey His Word, **do** His Word. Be open to and seek the process of sanctification.

✞ Forgive, forgive, forgive!

✞ Fight back against Satan! Exercise your authority as a believer!

✞ Give God all the glory! Share your testimony with the world! Be a witness for Christ! Go, spread God's Word, save souls, and make disciples!

When I started my blessed journey, I came to the Lord with childlike faith. Just as a young child totally trusts his earthly parents, I gave all of my trust to my heavenly Father. Just as a young child reaches up to his daddy with outstretched arms and says, "Pick me up, Daddy. Hold me!" I reached out to my heavenly Father and said, "Hold me, Father. Help me. I need You!" Just as a young child believes every word that comes forth from his parents' mouths, I believed every single word of God, given to me in His Bible. Just as a child obeys his parents out of trust and respect, I obeyed my heavenly Father out of deep reverence and trust that He loves me and knows best what I need.

I surrendered my whole self to Him, 100 percent. I held nothing back. I relinquished control to Him of every area of my life. I reached out to Him, and He received me into His

Kingdom with a mighty, powerful love. I never looked back. I never doubted the reality and truth of my God. I ventured forward, steadily and with my whole heart turned upward to Him. Since the day I was saved, I have hungered to grow in my relationship with my Father, to seek His face, to hear His voice.

## I'M SOLD OUT TO MY GOD!

The rest of this book is an itinerary for you to follow to receive the same results that I received ... total, complete healing of body, mind, and spirit! I will go into depth to share with you each of the steps of the journey I took. I encourage you to take these steps as well ... all the way to your own divine healing!

# Chapter Twenty-one

# SURRENDER

The first and <u>most absolutely critical step</u> in God's plan for you is to surrender your life to Him. The Bible repeatedly talks about salvation and how to receive salvation. Take time to meditate on the following scriptures. Read them slowly. Let them penetrate deep into your heart.

*The Lord is my light and my salvation – whom shall I fear? The Lord is the stronghold of my life – of whom shall I be afraid?* (Psalm 27:1 NIV).

*Yet to all who received him, to those who believed in his name, he gave the right to become children of God – children born not of natural descent, nor of human decision or a husband's will, but born of God* (John 1:12-13 NIV).

In the following scripture from the Gospel of John, Jesus teaches a Pharisee named Nicodemus about being born again:

*In reply Jesus declared, "I tell you the truth, no one can see the kingdom of God unless he is born again."*

*"How can a man be born when he is old?" Nicodemus asked. "Surely he cannot enter a second time into his mother's womb to be born!"*

*Jesus answered, "I tell you the truth, no one can enter the kingdom of God unless he is born of water and the Spirit. Flesh gives birth to flesh, but the Spirit gives birth to spirit. You should not be surprised at my saying, 'You must be born again.' The wind blows wherever it pleases. You hear its sound, but you cannot tell where it comes from or where it is going. So it is with everyone born of the Spirit."*

*"How can this be?" Nicodemus asked . . .*

*"Just as Moses lifted up the snake in the desert, so the Son of Man must be lifted up, that everyone who believes in him may have eternal life. For God so loved the world that he gave his one and only Son, that whoever believes in him shall not perish but have eternal life"* (John 3:3-9,14-16 NIV).

*"Salvation is found in no one else [except Jesus], for there is no other name under heaven given to men by which we must be saved"* (Acts 4:12 NIV).

*This righteousness from God comes through faith in Jesus Christ to all who believe. There is no difference, for all have sinned and fall short of the glory of God, and are justified freely by his grace through the redemption that came by Christ Jesus* (Romans 3:22-24 NIV).

*At one time we too were foolish, disobedient, deceived and enslaved by all kinds of passions and pleasures. We lived in malice and envy, being hated and hating one another. But when the kindness and love of God our Savior appeared, he saved us, not because of righteous things we had done, but because of his mercy. He saved us through the washing of rebirth and renewal by the*

*Holy Spirit, whom he poured out on us generously through Jesus Christ our Savior, so that, having been justified by his grace, we might become heirs having the hope of eternal life* (Titus 3:3-7 NIV).

*And this is the testimony: God has given us eternal life, and this life is in his Son. He who has the Son has life; he who does not have the Son of God does not have life* (1 John 5:11-12 NIV).

It is made crystal clear through God's Word regarding salvation and new birth, that there is only one way to salvation, and that is through our personal faith in Jesus Christ, through the grace of our compassionate God.

> **WHAT IS FAITH, AND HOW DO I EXERCISE IT IN ORDER TO RECEIVE MY SALVATION?**

<u>Faith for salvation means absolutely, firmly believing with all our heart in Jesus Christ, and all that the Bible teaches about Him. It means yielding our will and surrendering our total selves to Jesus Christ.</u> When we surrender to Jesus, we hold back nothing.

In the world in which we live, it is perceived as "strong" or "powerful" to handle difficult situations with ease, to assert your personal skills and intelligence to achieve success. But when we surrender to Jesus, we come before Him with humility, not with pride. We see Him as above all and in control of all; above and in control of our career and our success; above and in control of our relationships; above and in control of our health. Perhaps that's why it's so common for people to come to the Lord as they are living through desperate situations, as I was with cancer. It makes sense to surrender when you don't know what else to do, when you simply don't know how to handle your problems with your own human resources.

But, when everything's going great, it may be a different story. WE want to take all the credit for our success. We do NOT want to humble ourselves before God, giving Him all the honor and glory for the blessings we possess. The world says that we should be proud of ourselves; our talents, abilities, efforts, and resulting payoffs. But the Word says those who exalt themselves will be humbled, and those who humble themselves will be exalted. The results of humbling ourselves and of surrendering to Jesus are not demeaning in any way. The results of surrendering to Jesus are glorious!

The ability to experience His love in your life far outweighs the "power" you may have felt as a self-righteous overachiever. We constantly hear and read about famous, rich, successful people who are totally miserable. That's because there is simply no way to be fulfilled, **except through Jesus Christ**!

Paul prayed this prayer for the Ephesians, and it is also for you and me – a prayer to be <u>truly fulfilled</u> through the love of Christ: *May He grant you out of the rich treasury of His glory to be strengthened and reinforced with mighty power in the inner man by the [Holy] Spirit [Himself indwelling your innermost being and personality]. May Christ through your faith [actually] dwell (settle down, abide, make His permanent home) in your hearts! May you be rooted deep in love and founded securely on love. That you may have the power and be strong to apprehend and grasp with all the saints [God's devoted people, the experience of that love] what is the breadth and length and height and depth [of it]: [That you may really come] to know [practically, through experience for yourselves] the love of Christ, which far surpasses mere knowledge [without experience];* **that you may be filled [through all your being] unto all the fullness of God [may have the richest measure of the divine Presence, and become a body wholly filled and flooded with God Himself]!** (Ephesians 3:16-19 AMP).

<u>Faith for salvation also involves repentance ... turning away from sin and toward God through Christ.</u> Repentance includes sorrow for our old way of life, and a desire to change, to grow into the new creation God speaks about in 2 Corinthians 5:17: *Therefore, if anyone is in Christ, he is a new creation; old things have passed away; behold, all things have become new.*

The very second that you surrender your life to God and ask Jesus into your heart, you become a born-again child of God. As God's child, the seeds of the fruit of the Spirit are planted within you (love, joy, peace, longsuffering, gentleness, goodness, faith, meekness, and temperance). With the help of the Holy Spirit, you can cultivate these seeds. You can mature and develop your godly character your whole life long.

As the Bible teaches, our part in salvation is faith; absolute belief in Jesus Christ, surrender, repentance, and a desire to change and to grow in the ways of the Lord. And God's part is His amazing grace!

## What is Grace?

Grace is a gift, unmerited or undeserved, given through the love of our Father. It is not something we can earn through works. *For it is by grace you have been saved, through faith – and this not from yourselves, it is the gift of God – not by works, so that no one can boast* (Ephesians 2:8-9 NIV). We are totally dependent upon God's grace, His tender mercies, His lovingkindness, His forgiveness. We deserve spiritual death, separation from God forever, but through God's grace we are given spiritual life – life in the presence and in the glory of God! And that was made possible through Jesus, our Savior, *Who was betrayed and put to death because of our misdeeds and was raised to secure our justification (our acquittal), [making our account balance and absolving us from all guilt before God]* (Romans 4:25 AMP). Jesus paid the price for us, that we might be redeemed of sin and eternal death, and have abundant life, both in this world and in the world to come! Hallelujah!

## Exactly how do I receive this incredible gift of salvation?

Okay, so the two components required for salvation are <u>our faith</u> in Jesus Christ and <u>God's grace</u>.

*"The word is near you; it is in your mouth and in your heart," that is, the word of faith we are proclaiming: That if you confess with your mouth, "Jesus is Lord," and believe in your heart that God raised him from the dead, you will be saved. For it is with your heart that you believe and are justified, and it is with your*

*mouth that you confess and are saved. As the Scripture says, "Anyone who trusts in him will never be put to shame." For there is no difference between Jew and Gentile — the same Lord is Lord of all and richly blesses all who call on him, for, "Everyone who calls on the name of the Lord will be saved"* (Romans 10:8-13 NIV).

Two parts of our body are involved in receiving salvation: our heart and our mouth! It is <u>with our heart</u> that we believe, that we surrender, that we repent, and that we desire to change, to grow up spiritually, and to follow the lordship of Jesus Christ. But the Word also says that we must <u>use our mouth</u> to invite Jesus into our life and to confess "Jesus is Lord"!

If you have never taken this awesome step before, please stop right now and invite Jesus into your life. I'm including a simple prayer of salvation if you want to use it. Read it out loud with utter sincerity. Or just talk to God directly from your heart. The exact words aren't important. But your salvation IS more important than words can possibly say. It is your redemption from sin, sickness, and poverty. It is your eternal life!

# Prayer of Salvation

Heavenly Father, I believe Your Word that says, "Whosoever shall call on the name of the Lord shall be saved" and "If you confess with your mouth the Lord Jesus, and believe in your heart that God has raised Him from the dead, you shall be saved" (Acts 2:21; Romans 10:9). You said my salvation would be the result of Your Holy Spirit giving me new birth by coming to live in me (John 3:5-6,14-16; Romans 8:9-11).

Father, I'm asking You now for salvation, for new birth. I desperately want You and need You in my life. I believe with all my heart that Jesus is Your Son and that He died on the cross for me. I am sorry for my sins, Lord God. Please forgive me for them and create a clean heart in me. I open the door of my heart and say, YES, I receive Jesus as my Savior, and I choose to follow Him as the Lord of my life!

Father, I surrender to You completely, with all of my heart and soul. I surrender my health to You. I surrender my mind, my will, and my emotions to You. Grow me up strong, Father, from the inside out. I hunger for completeness through You. I trust You, Lord, with all of my heart, and I relinquish control of my life to You. I declare that I am Your child, and that I will obey You as my heavenly Father.

I thank You, my Father, for Your love so great, so precious, that You have provided for me a life of abundance. I reach out to You, Lord, and receive all that You have planned for me! And

I praise You, Who are so worthy to be praised! I love You more than words can possibly express. And You love me!

I declare that right now I am a child of God. I am free from sin and full of the righteousness of God. I am saved in Jesus' name! Amen! Glory be to God!

## Chapter Twenty-two

# THE PROMISE

*G*od has promised you another incredible gift, the baptism of the Holy Spirit. Jesus made a promise to us when He was on this earth. In John 14:15-17 Jesus said, *"If you love Me, keep My commandments. And I will pray the Father, and He will give you another Helper, that He may abide with you forever – the Spirit of truth, whom the world cannot receive, because it neither sees Him nor knows Him; but you know Him, for He dwells with you and will be in you. I will not leave you orphans; I will come to you.*

Later in the same gospel, Jesus tells us, *"These things I have spoken to you while being present with you. But the Helper, the Holy Spirit, whom the Father will send in My name, He will teach you all things, and bring to your remembrance all things that I said to you"* (John 14:25-26).

Right before Jesus ascended into heaven, forty days after His resurrection from the grave, Jesus was assembled with His people. He told them, *"Behold, I send the Promise of My Father upon you; but tarry in the city of Jerusalem until you are **endued with power from on high**"* (Luke 24:49). Again in the book of Acts, it says: *And being assembled together with them, He* *commanded them not to depart from Jerusalem, but to wait for the Promise of the Father, "which," He said, "you have heard from Me; for John truly baptized with water, but you shall be baptized with the Holy Spirit not many days from now . . . But **you shall receive power** when the Holy Spirit has come upon you; and **you shall be witnesses** to Me in Jerusalem, and in all Judea and Samaria, and to the end of the earth"* (Acts 1:4-5,8).

One hundred and twenty people gathered in the upper room to wait for the Promise. The apostles, Mary the mother of Jesus, and Jesus' brothers were all there, along with many more followers of Jesus Christ. They spent their waiting time in fervent corporate prayer and supplication (a humble, earnest request).

*When the Day of Pentecost had fully come, they were all with one accord in one place. And suddenly there came a sound from heaven, as of a rushing mighty wind, and it filled the whole house where they were sitting. Then there appeared to them divided tongues, as of fire, and one sat upon each of them. And they were all filled with the Holy Spirit and began to speak with other tongues, as the Spirit gave them utterance* (Acts 2:1-4).

The crowd witnessing this event had mixed reactions. Some were amazed and marveled at the outward evidence of the baptism of the Holy Spirit. But others mocked the believers saying, *They are full of new wine* (Acts 2:13). At that point Peter, endued with power from on high, stood up and gave a great sermon to explain what had happened to them.

Following his teaching, the people *were cut to the heart, and said to Peter and the rest of the apostles, "Men and brethren, what shall we do?" Then Peter said to them, "Repent, and let every one of you be baptized in the name of Jesus Christ for the remission of sins;* **and you shall receive the gift of the Holy Spirit. For the promise is to you and to your children, and to all who are afar off, as many as the Lord our God will call.**" *And with many other words he testified and exhorted them, saying, "Be saved from this perverse generation." Then those who gladly received his word were baptized; and that day about* **three thousand souls were added to them** (Acts 2:37-41).

This scripture is so rich. It is a blueprint of what God has in store for us! It shows us how Peter, with the infilling of the Holy Spirit, was endued with power from on high. His preaching and teaching led 3,000 people to the Lord following his first anointed sermon! And through the inspiration of the Holy Spirit, he tells you and me that the Promise is also for us! *"And you shall receive the gift of the Holy Spirit. For the promise is to you and to your children, and to all who are afar off, as many as the Lord our God will call"* (Acts 2:38-39).

---

### WHAT ARE THE BENEFITS OF BEING BAPTIZED IN THE HOLY SPIRIT?

---

✞ The baptism in the Holy Spirit will bring personal boldness and power of the Spirit into the believer's life in order that he can accomplish mighty works in Christ's name, and so that he can be a more effective witness for Christ.

✞ The baptism in the Holy Spirit will give us a greater desire to pray.

✞ The baptism in the Holy Spirit will give us a deeper love and understanding of the Word.

✝ The baptism in the Holy Spirit will enhance our sensitivity to sin.

> ## But what about speaking in tongues?
> ## Is that for us too?

The answer is YES! If you look at two more sets of scriptures in the book of Acts, you will see that every single time people received the baptism of the Holy Spirit, they <u>always</u> spoke in tongues. Acts 10 accounts how the Holy Spirit fell upon a group of Gentiles, with the Bible evidence of speaking in tongues. And Acts 19 tells about twelve disciples at Ephesus receiving the baptism of the Holy Spirit and speaking in tongues. In every instance in the Bible, tongues accompany the baptism of the Holy Spirit.

> ## What is speaking in tongues all about?

Speaking in tongues involves the human spirit and the Spirit of God intermingling so the believer communicates directly to God at the level of his spirit rather than at the level of his mind. In the fourteenth chapter of the first book of Corinthians, Paul is teaching the church how and when to use their gift of tongues. *For if I pray in a tongue, my spirit prays, but my understanding is unfruitful. What is the conclusion then? I will pray with the spirit, and I will also pray with the understanding. I will sing with the spirit, and I will also sing with the understanding* (1 Corinthians 14:14-15).

I would suggest that you take time to read 1 Corinthians 14. If Paul found it necessary to write an entire chapter to the church of Corinth to bring order to the service in regards to tongues, it is clear evidence that many believers were baptized in the Holy Spirit with the Bible evidence of speaking in tongues!

---

**WHY SHOULD WE SPEAK IN TONGUES?**

---

✝ When we pray in tongues, we pray the perfect will of God. There are times when we don't know the will of God, times when we don't know how to pray for a situation. At these times, praying in the Spirit is the perfect prayer. *Likewise the Spirit also helps in our weaknesses. For we do not know what we should pray for as we ought, but the Spirit Himself makes intercession for us with groanings which cannot be uttered. Now He who searches the hearts knows what the mind of the Spirit is, because He makes intercession for the saints according to the will of God* (Romans 8:26-27).

✝ Speaking in tongues is speaking the mysteries of Christ. *For he who speaks in a tongue does not speak to men but to God, for no one understands him; however, in the spirit he speaks mysteries* (1 Corinthians 14:2). All the treasures of wisdom and knowledge are in Christ. When we speak in tongues, revelation about our inheritance in Christ comes to our spirit and enlightens our minds.

✝ Speaking in tongues is a means of magnifying God. *Then they were all amazed and marveled, saying to one another, "Look, are not all these who speak Galileans? And how is it that we hear, each in our own language in* *which we were born? … we hear them speaking in our own tongues **the wonderful works of God***" (Acts 2:7-8,11). *While Peter was still speaking these words, the Holy Spirit fell upon all those who heard the word. And those of the circumcision who believed were astonished, as many as came with Peter, because the gift of the Holy Spirit had been poured out on the Gentiles also. For they heard them speak with tongues and **magnify God*** (Acts 10:44-46).

✞ Speaking in tongues brings spiritual edification to the believer. Paul writes, *He who speaks in a tongue edifies himself* (1 Corinthians 14:4).

✞ Praying in tongues energizes the faith that God has already placed within us. *But you, beloved, **building yourselves up on your most holy faith**, praying in the Holy Spirit, keep yourselves in the love of God, looking for the mercy of our Lord Jesus Christ unto eternal life* (Jude 20-21).

✞ Satan can't understand tongues!

---

### How do we receive the baptism of the Holy Spirit, with the Bible evidence of speaking in other tongues?

---

There are four conditions for receiving the baptism of the Holy Spirit promised to us in God's Word.

1. You must be a born-again child of God.
2. You must have a sincere desire for the baptism of the Holy Spirit.

3. You must have an expectation or belief that you <u>will</u> <u>receive</u> God's gift. *"Therefore I say to you, whatever things you ask when you pray, believe that you receive them, and you will have them"* (Mark 11:24).

4. You must ask! *So I say to you, Ask and keep on asking and it shall be given you; seek and keep on seeking and you shall find; knock and keep on knocking and the door shall be opened to you. For everyone who asks and keeps on asking receives; and he who seeks and keeps on seeking finds; and to him who knocks and keeps on knocking, the door shall be opened. What father among you, if his son asks for a loaf of bread, will give him a stone; or if he asks for a fish, will instead of a fish give him a serpent? Or if he asks for an egg, will give him a scorpion? If you then, evil as you are, know how to give good gifts [gifts that are to their advantage] to your children,* **how much more will your heavenly Father give the Holy Spirit to those who ask and continue to ask Him!** (Luke 11:9-13 AMP).

After you pray and ask for this gift, you must supply your will and your vocal cords. The Holy Spirit will supply the manner of style by which you speak. If there is no effort to speak on your part, the Holy Spirit cannot and will not supply the utterance.

# Prayer for Baptism of the Holy Spirit

Father, Your Word says that the Holy Spirit is a gift. I do not have to work for it. All I need to do is ask and receive it. So I ask You, Jesus, come and baptize me with the Holy Spirit. I desire Your impartation in every part of my life. Lord, I want to receive all that You have for me!

My heart cry is for a radical transformation in my walk with You. Consume me, O God, with Your holy fire! I receive, right now, as an act of my will and my faith, the baptism of the Holy Spirit with the Bible evidence of speaking with other tongues.

Now take a deep breath and begin to speak forth in your heavenly language. Do not allow the enemy to tell you that you can't pray in tongues, because you can! Hallelujah! Continue to thank the Lord, to pour out your love for Him, to worship Him. Magnify Him with your heavenly language!

## Chapter Twenty-three

# RELATIONSHIP, NOT RELIGION

The topic of this chapter changed my life. First of all, I am alive, whole, and healthy. But I have so much more than just physical health. I have a wonderful, intimate relationship with my heavenly Father. In order to show you what I now have, I need to show you what I didn't have before. I need to contrast my old life with a strong religious background to my new life with a living, breathing, alive relationship with the Lord.

Before I was diagnosed with cancer, I considered myself a good person with a very strong faith. Our family went to church religiously every Sunday. We consistently took our children to religious education. I taught catechism when our kids were young. I even taught in a Catholic school for four years. I was a moral, law-abiding person. I was diligent and hardworking as a mother, homemaker, and teacher. But I never read the Bible. I seldom prayed. When I did pray, I prayed to a distant God. I did not talk to Him as my friend, my helper, my healer, my provider, my peace.

Most often, during church, I neither listened attentively to the scripture readings nor to the sermon. I rarely remembered what had been taught, and even more rarely applied any of it to my life. I put very little into my spiritual development, and thus got very little out of my "religious" experience. Please note that it wasn't God's lack, it was totally mine.

But now I have a close relationship with my Father. I come boldly before His throne into His holy presence. I minister to Him with praise for who He is and for what He does. I pour out my love to Him and welcome His loving-kindness and tender mercies. I present my requests to Him, with thanksgiving, and I **know** that He hears and answers my prayers. I feed on His living Word. It nourishes me, it sustains me, and it builds me up. I listen to His voice, spoken to me through His Word, and through the still small voice of the Holy Spirit within me. And it is my sincere longing to <u>do</u> what He tells me, to follow where He leads. My greatest desire is to grow closer to my God every day of my life.

*Seek me, inquire for, and require Me [as a vital necessity], and you will find Me when you search for Me with all of your heart* (Jeremiah 29:13 AMP). I love this scripture! God IS a vital necessity. He is THE vital necessity. My God is the very air that I breathe. He is the blood that courses through my veins. I need Him more than the water that I drink, or the food that I eat. He is my everything. He is all that I need and all that I want. And here's the best news of all; when you seek Him with all of your heart, you will find Him too!

If you've prayed the prayer of salvation and been baptized in the Holy Spirit, this is the next step on your journey. **Develop your relationship with your Father!** Start by setting a daily appointment with Him, and make a commitment to keep that appointment! The Word says that your appointment should be in the morning:

- ✞ Psalm 63:1 says: *O God, You are my God; early will I seek You; my soul thirsts for You; my flesh longs for You in a dry and thirsty land where there is no water.*
- ✞ Psalm 88:13 says: *But to You I have cried out, O Lord, and in the morning my prayer comes before You.*
- ✞ Jesus Himself gives us the perfect example of when to pray: *Now in the morning, having risen a long while before daylight, He went out and departed to a solitary place; and there He prayed* (Mark 1:35).

Of course, I agree with every word in the Bible, but let me tell you why I agree so fervently. Life is busy. Life is full of things to do and places to go. Life is unpredictable. As soon as we step out of bed, we typically begin our list for the day. And once we are in the midst of that list, it's not uncommon for more items to be added to our agenda, packing our day with too much to do and not enough time to do it in. Sound familiar? And now we need to find time to fellowship with God in there somewhere. Spending time with God shouldn't be at the end of our list of things to do. He should be our first priority!

Now rewind that scene. This time, set your alarm a little bit earlier, and start your day by praising God and pouring out your love to Him, by feeding on His living Word and by lifting up your anxieties to the Lord, casting all your cares upon Him, and trusting Him to direct your day. The peace of the Lord takes the place of the worry, and you start, continue, and end your day with the Lord in control, not puny old you! What a great deal!

How much time should you allot to your daily appointment with your Father? Don't be legalistic about the time you spend or the way that you spend it. But I guarantee that the biggest problem you'll have is closing your Bible, ending your prayer, and going off to continue your day. I would suggest that you give yourself at least thirty minutes to start, with leeway to have an hour or more if you desire. Of course, God is always available, so feel free to approach Him at any time: morning, noon, and night.

There are three distinct areas I'd like to reflect on regarding this fellowship time with the Lord: praise and worship, reading the Bible, and prayer.

## PRAISE AND WORSHIP

I never praised and worshipped God in my "religious" days. I sang songs, I said words, but they weren't songs and words from me to God. I wasn't giving Him glory for His creation, for His provisions, for His power, for the mighty God that He is. And I wasn't expressing my love for Him. As you develop your relationship with the Lord, developing a praising lifestyle is part of your spiritual growth. In this lifestyle, we desire to please God, we have a sincere attitude of appreciation, a sensitivity to the heart of God, and a commitment to express our love and appreciation to Him.

As a group unites to praise God, it is an awesome expression. My husband and I love to attend Christian concerts, where thousands of people who love God come together to praise Him. It is an awesome experience to be in the midst of that power of praise. But even in that setting, it is each individual blending as one, expressing their praise and adoration from their heart directly to God.

Praise means to commend; to applaud; to express approval or admiration of; to extol in words or in song; to magnify; to glorify. We can praise God through written music or through improvisation. We can praise Him in song or simply with spoken words. We can praise Him through shouting, making a joyful noise, through musical instruments, dancing, and through lifting our hands. I witnessed all of the above the first time I stepped into the church I am now a member of. Remember when I had hands laid on me by the faith healer the day that the intense pain left my body? The day when I stood through the praise and worship, watching the abandonment of the people as they openly expressed their love for God? I don't just watch anymore; I praise God with all my heart and soul!

One question that is often asked is, "Why do you lift your hands?" First of all, lifting our hands in praise is scriptural.

✝ *And Ezra blessed the Lord, the great God. Then all the people answered, "Amen, Amen!" while lifting up their hands. And they bowed their heads and worshiped the Lord with their faces to the ground* (Nehemiah 8:6).

✝ *I desire therefore that the men pray everywhere, lifting up holy hands, without wrath and doubting* (1 Timothy 2:8).

✝ *Hear the voice of my supplications when I cry to You, when I lift up my hands toward Your holy sanctuary* (Psalm 28:2).

✝ *Thus I will bless You while I live; I will lift up my hands in Your name* (Psalm 63:4).

✝ *Lift up your hands in the sanctuary, and bless the Lord* (Psalm 134:2).

When we lift our hands in praise of our Lord, it is a form of greeting and embrace, much like a small child lifts his hands to his mother to say, "Mommy, pick me up, hold me close, love me!" As we lift our hands to the Lord, we get more focused on the Lord in our praise and worship. When we lift up our hands, we are vulnerable and open to surrender to the Lord. We lift our hands symbolically to receive everything that God has for us!

Praise ushers in worship. Praise sings <u>about</u> God; worship sings <u>to</u> God. Worship is walking in intimacy with God. It is the first and principal purpose of our eternal calling. Worship is giving our total selves to God, expressing our love and adoration to Him with an acknowledgement of His supremacy and lordship. Worship is an unashamed pouring out of our inner self upon the Lord Jesus in affectionate devotion. When I worship, even in a crowd of thousands at a Christian concert, it is just me and God. Worship is to God, for God, and about God. It's not about what I feel or receive, even though I often do experience His presence and receive a special touch of His love and His precious peace. Worship is all about us giving to God what He is so very worthy of.

So how does this fit into your daily appointment with God? Simply take time to praise Him for who He is, thank Him for what He has done for you, and express your love to Him. Use words or music or song or dance or whatever expression fits your style and personality. He knows your heart, and that's what is so important.

## READING THE BIBLE

Another nonnegotiable in developing your relationship with your Father is reading the Bible, God's living Word, given to you! Just as your body requires nourishment to strengthen you and stay in good health, you need spiritual food to keep you strong spiritually and in good spiritual health! In the sixth chapter of John, Jesus teaches us that He is the Bread of Life. *And Jesus said to them, "I am the bread of life. He who comes to Me shall never hunger, and he who believes in Me shall never thirst . . . The words that I speak to you are spirit, and they are life"* (John 6:35,63).

Proverbs 4 clearly teaches the life-giving power of the Word. *"Lay hold of my words with all your heart; keep my commands and you will live ... Listen, my son, accept what I say, and the years of your life will be many . . . Hold on to instruction, do not let it go: guard it well, for it is your life . . . My son, pay attention to what I say: listen closely to my words. Do not let them out of your sight, keep them within your heart: for they are life to those who find them and health to a man's whole body* (Proverbs 4:4,10,13,20-22 NIV). Psalm 119, the longest book in the Bible, is about the written

Word of God, its power and its wonder, the importance of feeding on the Word and doing the Word! Take time to read and meditate on this Psalm.

The Bible is God's divinely inspired Word, His love letter to us! *Every Scripture is God-breathed (given by His inspiration) and profitable for instruction, for reproof and conviction of sin, for correction of error and discipline in obedience, [and] for training in righteousness (in holy living, in conformity to God's will in thought, purpose, and action), so that the man of God may be complete and proficient, well fitted and thoroughly equipped for every good work* (2 Timothy 3:16-17 AMP).

*For the Word that God speaks is alive and full of power [making it active, operative, energizing, and effective]; it is sharper than any two-edged sword, penetrating to the dividing line of the breath of life (soul) and [the immortal] spirit, and of joints and marrow [of the deepest parts of our nature], exposing and sifting and analyzing and judging the very thoughts and purposes of the heart* (Hebrews 4:12 AMP). We desperately <u>need</u> the Word in order to be equipped to live our Christian life!

Here are four steps to get the most possible out of your time spent in the Word.

✝ **First, approach the Word with prayer.** Paul prayed a wonderful prayer for the people of Ephesus. But the Word of God is just as alive for you as it was in the original letters. This is Paul's prayer personalized for you. "I keep asking that the God of our Lord Jesus Christ, the glorious Father, may give me the Spirit of wisdom and revelation, so that I may know Him better. I pray also that the eyes of my heart may be enlightened as I read and meditate on God's Word, in order that I may know the hope to which He has called me, the riches of His glorious inheritance in the saints, and His incomparably great power for us who believe!" (This is not a direct quotation from the Bible. It is a paraphrase of Ephesians 1:17-19 NIV.) Praying this scripture is an excellent way to begin your daily time in the Word.

✞ **Second, read the Word slowly and carefully.** Try reading the Word out loud, allowing it to enter your ears, your mind, and move into your heart. Where should you begin reading? I suggest starting with the Gospel of John, which is John's version of the life of Jesus, and His magnificent teaching. Then read Acts, which tells of the beginning of the Church, and the power given to God's disciples (that includes you!) to witness and to do God's work! Then read the epistles, the letters written by Paul to the various churches of that era. These letters are wonderful sermons or teachings that apply directly to us as believers!

✞ **Third, meditate on the Word.** When a scripture or passage speaks to you personally, take it out and chew on it for a while. Reread it. Recite it. You may even want to commit it to memory. Think about how it applies to your life. Pray about it if it is an area you need to work on or if the Word has brought conviction to you regarding your own life. Look up the scripture or passage and read it in different translations. (Biblegateway.com is a good resource to look up scriptures in various translations.)

✠ **Fourth, put God's Word into action.** Do His Word; live it. Look back at Hebrews 4:12 AMP: [God's Word] *is sharper than any two-edged sword ... exposing and sifting and analyzing and judging the very thoughts and purposes of the heart.* Once the thoughts and purposes of our hearts have been exposed and analyzed and judged through the Word, it is our responsibility to do something about it! Thank God we have the Holy Spirit to help us! *I have strength for all things in Christ Who empowers me [I am ready for anything and equal to anything through Him Who infuses inner strength into me; I am self-sufficient in Christ's sufficiency]* (Philippians 4:13 AMP).

The more Word you put in, the more you have to draw on for strength. We need good food for energy and physical strength to sustain us. You don't just eat once or twice a week. You must eat healthy meals consistently, three times a day, every day. You need the Word consistently too! It is your spiritual food, your nourishment, your sustenance! A little Word equals a little nourishment; a lot of Word equals a lot of nourishment! *Out of the abundance of the heart his mouth speaks* (Luke 6:45).

As you read the Word and it becomes a part of you, the Holy Spirit will bring it to your remembrance when you have a need for it. And the more Word that you have in you, the more readily the Holy Spirit can draw it out of you, both for your needs and in order to minister to others! Isn't that awesome?

## PRAYER

The third area in which to develop your relationship with your Father is through prayer. What is prayer? First, let me clarify what prayer is NOT. Prayer is NOT trying to get God's attention. You already HAVE God's attention! Prayer is NOT trying to get God to do something. He's already done it! But prayer IS communing with God – believing you receive what He has already given to you in Christ Jesus! *His divine power has given us everything we need for life and godliness through our knowledge of him who called us by his own glory and goodness. Through these he has given us his very great and precious promises* (the Word), *so that through them you may participate in the divine nature and escape the corruption in the world caused by evil desires* (2 Peter 1:3-4 NIV). Prayer is the turning of the human soul to the living God. Prayer is the greatest power in the world!

There are three common phases we go through as we start a prayer life. At first, you will desire to have a prayer life. When you invite Jesus into your life and receive the baptism of the Holy Spirit, you will truly desire this intimate time with your Father. However, as you get started, you'll notice that you need to discipline your flesh to make time and take time to pray. You may not always "feel" like praying. Do NOT go by feelings. You don't need to "feel" God in order to be communing with Him. The third phase is delight! As you begin to spend more and more time in prayer, the delight of spending time with God becomes your motivation. Prayer becomes something you do out of a deep love and desire to spend time with your Father.

What do you say when you pray? The eloquence of your prayer is not what is important. The sincerity of your heart is what God hears. The more you experience conversational prayer, the easier and more fluent you will become. Here is a very general guide to help you to focus your prayer.

☩ Begin with praising God for who He is: your Lord, your Savior, your Healer, your Comforter, your Advocate, your Helper, your Peace, etc.

☩ Thank Him for what He has done for you.

☩ Express your sincere love and devotion to Him.

☩ Confess your sins, and forgive others.

☩ Surrender every area of your life to the Lord, and entrust Him to take control!

☩ Make your requests of God for your needs, or for the needs of others.

☩ Bind Satan from your life and the life of your loved ones.

☩ Close your prayer time with praise once again.

Remember that praying in tongues has many benefits. Spend time praying in tongues daily as well as in your understanding. You will be abundantly blessed!

The next chapter is going to continue with direction in this important area of your faith journey. We will look closely at how to pray effectively, the prayer of faith, the power of praying the Word, and the power of our own words.

## Chapter Twenty-four

# THE PRAYER OF FAITH

There is effective prayer and ineffective prayer. As we go back to those two difficult questions – Why are some people healed, but not others? and Why do bad things happen to good people? – praying effectively is a critical factor.

The Word teaches us to pray to the Father in the name of Jesus. Jesus Himself expressed this principle when He said, *"Most assuredly, I say to you, whatever you ask the Father in My name He will give you. Until now you have asked nothing in My name. Ask, and you will receive, that your joy may be full"* (John 16:23-24). And in John 14:13-14 Jesus says, *"And whatever you ask in My name, that I will do, that the Father may be glorified in the Son. If you ask anything in My name, I will do it."* Not only does Jesus tell us how to pray, He also guarantees us that our prayers will be answered! I personally stand on that Word and believe its truth!

Thus, **the first factor in effective prayer is that when you pray, make your requests of the Father, but ask in the name of Jesus.** Let me give you an example. If I were to pray for safe travel for my sons, I might pray like this: "Dear heavenly Father, I pray now for my boys. You tell me in Philippians 4:6-7 to be anxious for nothing, but in everything, with prayer and supplication, with thanksgiving, let our requests be made known to You, and Your peace, which passes all understanding, will guard our hearts and minds through Christ Jesus. So I lift my boys to you now, <u>Father God</u>, and ask You to protect them as they travel. Send Your ministering angels to surround them with Your mighty hedge of protection. I cast this care upon You, <u>Father</u>. I trust You with all my heart, and I receive Your peace that passes all understanding. <u>I ask this in the name of Jesus.</u> Thank You! Amen! So be it!"

**The second critical factor in effective prayer is that you must have a sincere, true faith, or belief that your prayer will be answered!** Read these next two sentences very slowly:

The world says "seeing is believing."
The Word says "believing is seeing!"

Throughout the Bible, when we see Jesus' miraculous healings, He required two things: pure hearts free from sin (which will be the focus of the next chapter) and faith! In Mark 9, there is an account of a father who comes to Jesus to request healing for his son who had a mute spirit. *Then they brought him* [the boy] *to Him* [Jesus] *… the spirit convulsed him, and he fell on the ground and wallowed, foaming at the mouth. So He* [Jesus] *asked his father, "How long has this been happening to him?" And he said, "From childhood. And often he has thrown him both into the fire and into the water to destroy him. But if You can do anything, have compassion on us and help us." Jesus said to him, "If you can believe, all things are possible to him who believes." Immediately the father of the child cried out and said with tears. "Lord, I believe; help my unbelief!"* (Mark 9:20-24). Then Jesus healed the boy.

We must believe, without doubt, in order to receive! This next scripture is foundational in the teaching of faith, and it is taught to us directly from our Lord Jesus Christ.

*"Have faith in God. For assuredly, I say to you, whoever says to this mountain, 'Be removed and be cast into the sea,' and does not doubt in his heart, but believes that those things he says will be done, he will have whatever he says. Therefore I say to you, whatever things you ask when you pray, believe that you receive them, and you will have them.*

Mark 11:22-24

James 1:6-8 AMP tells us the consequence of doubting versus believing: *Only it must be in faith that he asks with no wavering (no hesitating, no doubting). For the one who wavers (hesitates, doubts) is like the billowing surge out at sea that is blown hither and thither and tossed by the wind. For truly,* **let not such a person imagine that he will receive anything [he asks for] from the Lord,** *{For being as he is] a man of two minds (hesitating, dubious, irresolute), [he is] unstable and unreliable and uncertain about everything [he thinks, feels, decides].*

Hebrews, chapter 11, is the "Faith Hall of Fame"! Read the whole chapter to see how mighty men and women of God exercised their faith, believing without doubt, and how their prayers were answered! The first verse of Hebrews 11 NIV defines faith: *Now faith is being sure of what we hope for and certain of what we do not see.* Hope is what we want and is in the future tense. But faith is a belief now that it is done, even though we may not see it!

God didn't promise us healing; he provided it for us through the death and resurrection of Jesus! It's already done! First Peter 2:24 tells us that healing belongs to us! *Who Himself bore our sins in His own body on the tree, that we, having died to sins, might live for righteousness –* **by whose stripes you were healed!** It is up to us to believe, to have faith in this truth!

Just as the father of the child with the mute spirit, we often say, "Lord, I believe," followed immediately by, "Help my unbelief"! How can we develop our faith and rid ourselves of doubt?

**Faith comes by hearing the Word of God.**
**Faith is released by speaking the Word of God.**
**Faith grows by doing the Word of God.**

**The third component of effectual prayer** relates directly to these three statements, so I will discuss them simultaneously. **In order for our prayers to be answered, they must be in the will of God.** First John 5:14-15 NIV says: *This is the confidence we have in approaching God: that if we ask anything **according to his will,** he hears us. And if we know that he hears us – whatever we ask – we know that we have what we asked of him.*

Again, look at God's guarantee. He doesn't say that we might have what we ask of Him. He says that if we ask anything according to His will, He hears us, and if we know that He hears us, whatever we ask, we know that we have what we asked of Him! The only variable in the equation is whether or not our prayer is according to the will of God. The rest is nonnegotiable! And the Word says that healing IS the will of God. Jesus healed ALL who were sick. *Jesus Christ is the same yesterday, today, and forever* (Hebrews 13:8). Therefore, it is unscriptural to pray, "If it be thy will, heal me," yet that is exactly how so many people pray for healing. How, then, should you pray for healing?

Pray using the Word of God, which is the absolute perfect will of God! Confessing (or saying) the Word of God serves two purposes. First, it is the perfect prayer, a powerful weapon, and will not come back void. Isaiah 55:11 says: *So shall My word be that goes forth from My mouth; it shall not return to Me void, but it shall accomplish what I please, and it shall prosper in the thing for which I sent it.* Second, hearing the Word of God will develop your faith, which is a requirement for healing! *So then faith comes by hearing, and hearing by the word of God* (Romans 10:17). Romans 10:8 says, *"The word is near you, in your mouth and in your heart"* (that is, the word of faith which we preach). Notice that first the Word of faith is in your mouth, then in your heart. Saying the Word of God enables the Word to move from your mouth to your ears, and into your heart, where it becomes a firm foundation of faith, a sturdy root which will grow into the fruit of healing!

Here is a sample of scriptural confessions that I pray regarding cancer. They are not direct quotations from the Bible; rather, they are paraphrased confessions based on the Scriptures noted.

- ✝ Jesus bore my sins in His body on the tree; therefore I am dead to sin and alive unto God and by His stripes I am healed and made whole (1 Peter 2:24).
- ✝ Jesus bore the curse for me; therefore I forbid melanoma from inhabiting my body. The life of God within me dissolves all melanoma, and my strength

and health are maintained (Matthew 16:19; John 14:13; Mark 11:23).

✟ Melanoma has no right to my body. It is a thing of the past for I have been delivered from the authority of darkness (Colossians 1:13-14).

✟ Heavenly Father, as I give voice to Your Word, the law of the Spirit of life in Christ Jesus makes me free from the law of sin and death. Your life is energizing every cell of my body (Romans 8:2).

✟ The same Spirit that raised Jesus from the dead dwells in me, permeating His life through my veins and sending healing throughout my body (Romans 8:11).

✟ You have forgiven all my iniquities. You have healed my body of cancer. You have redeemed my life from destruction. You have satisfied my mouth with good things so that my youth is renewed as the eagle (Psalm 103:2-5).

✟ Jesus gave me the authority to use His name. And that which I bind on earth is bound in heaven and that which I loose on earth is loosed in heaven. Therefore, I bind melanoma from my body; you are evicted from my body and cast out into the sea. I loose the healing power of God in my body now, in Jesus' name (Matthew 18:18).

✟ I will not die, but live, and declare the works of the Lord! (Psalm 118:17).

For a more complete set of healing confessions, I recommend the book that I use for my healing confessions, *God's Creative Power for Healing*, by Charles Capps. Take your daily confessions very seriously! This is the best medicine there is for any sickness! Say them aloud, with fervency, at least three times a day. If you are physically having a difficult time doing this, tape record your confessions, and listen to them constantly. The critical factor is that <u>you must hear the spoken Word of God</u> in order to build your faith.

You must also guard the way you speak. *Death and life are in the power of the tongue, and they who indulge in it shall eat the fruit of it [for death or life]* (Proverbs 18:21 AMP). The third chapter of James also talks about the power of the tongue. Verse 10 says: *Out of the same mouth proceed blessing and cursing. My brethren, these things ought not to be so.* We need to speak ONLY the blessing. In regards to healing, we need to speak the result, the healing for which Jesus paid the price, not the diagnosis or prognosis.

My diagnosis was Stage 4 melanoma, with metastasis throughout my lymphatic system. My prognosis was six to nine months to live. However, I spoke the results that I believed! In the privacy of my home, I claimed my healing, I cursed the cancer, and I stood on God's Word that I am the healed of the Lord! In public, I told people that I was doing excellent; that God was taking really good care of me. I did not claim the cancer. I NEVER called it "my cancer"; rather, I referred to it as the "diagnosis of cancer."

When I had physical symptoms or intense doubts, I rarely verbalized them. When I did, it was to receive support and strength from fellow believers or pastors through the prayer of agreement. Remember that one of the causes of sickness and disease in this world is the law of sowing and reaping. If you sow words of sickness and believe that you will receive sickness,

sickness is what you will reap. If you sow words of health and believe that you will receive healing, healing is what you will reap. God said, *"But the word is very near you, in your mouth and in your heart, that you may do it . . . I call heaven and earth as witnesses today against you, that I have set before you life and death, blessing and cursing; therefore choose life, that both you and your descendants may live* (Deuteronomy 30:14,19).

## I CHOOSE LIFE!

**The final step in effectual prayer is to step out in faith.** <u>Act</u> like you are healthy and whole. You may not physically feel like it, but do it anyway. Get up, take care of daily business. Declare your healing, and then act like it is so! It doesn't take faith to believe what you see. But it takes a mighty faith to believe a result you don't see or feel. Remember, a mature fruit begins with a seed. When planted in the fertile soil of your heart, and given the water of the Word, it sprouts and begins to take root. The stem and leaves grow, followed by a bud, a blossom, a baby fruit, and finally a mature fruit.

When you receive your healing, it begins with a seed of faith planted deep within your heart, and develops into the manifestation of complete healing! Be patient, be persistent, be absolutely confident, and stand firm in the truth and the power of the Word. You ARE healed. It is done, in the name of Jesus! Hallelujah!

## Chapter Twenty-five

# SANCTIFICATION

*L*et's go back once again to those two difficult questions: Why are some people healed but not others? and Why do bad things happen to good people? Remember also that one of the causes of sickness and disease is disobedience to the Word of God (Chapter 20, "Healing Is Conditional"). That leads us to the next critical step in God's plan: Not only must we pray the perfect will of God in order to receive our healing; **we must also be IN the perfect will of God!**

When we receive Jesus as our Lord and Savior, we become new creatures. By the grace of God, we are set free from sin's power and dominion. *For sin shall not [any longer] exert dominion over you, since now you are not under Law [as slaves], but under grace [as subjects of God's favor and mercy]* (Romans 6:14 AMP). Through the Holy Spirit within us, we are able not to sin, even though we never come to the place where we are free from temptation and the possibility of sin.

Sanctification is the process of developing your godly character; becoming holy, separated from the world, and set apart from sin so that you may have intimate fellowship with God and serve Him gladly! This is a lifelong process, and we may fall many times. But don't count those times as failures. Count them as practice!

Sanctification is part of God's plan for you – for your faith journey and for receiving God's healing. The Bible is your blueprint for holy living and obedience to God. Since every facet of God's plan is taught in the Word, let me share just a couple of powerful scripture passages regarding His plan of holiness for you.

*Since we have these promises, dear friends, let us purify ourselves from everything that contaminates body and spirit, perfecting holiness out of reverence for God* (2 Corinthians 7:1 NIV).

*Therefore, prepare your minds for action; be self-controlled; set your hope fully on the grace to be given you when Jesus Christ is revealed. As obedient children, do not conform to the evil desires you had when you lived in ignorance. But just as he who called you is holy, so be holy in all you do; for it is written: "Be holy, because I am holy"* (1 Peter 1:13-16 NIV).

What exactly does "being holy" entail? After all, we are only human! How can we ever be holy? Isn't that putting ourselves on the level of God where we never ever will be? NO! God Himself gave us instructions to be holy, and He wouldn't ask us to do something that wasn't possible for us to do! Holy living is living <u>without sin</u>. Holy living is more than just following the Ten Commandments. (This is where the "good people" often stop. They follow all of the "Thou shalts" and the "Thou shalt nots," but they don't continue on into developing their love walk.)

Holy living is also living the Great Commandment that Jesus gave to us. *"The first of all the commandments is: 'Hear, O Israel, the Lord our God, the Lord is one. And you shall love the Lord your God with all your heart, with all your soul, with all your mind, and with all your strength.' This is the first commandment. And the second, like it, is this: 'You shall love your neighbor as yourself.' There is no other commandment greater than these"* (Mark 12:29-31). The love walk is the path that leads you into a life of holiness. The following scripture from Colossians portrays the wide range of expectations God has for His saints, His set-apart ones.

*Since, then, you have been raised with Christ, set your hearts on things above, where Christ is seated at the right hand of God. Set your minds on things above, not on earthly things. For you died, and your life is now hidden with Christ in God. When Christ, who is your life, appears, then you also will appear with him in glory.*

*Put to death, therefore, whatever belongs to your earthly nature: sexual immorality, impurity, lust, evil desires and greed, which is idolatry. Because of these, the wrath of God is coming. You used to walk in these ways, in the life you once lived. But now you must rid yourselves of all such things as these: anger, rage, malice, slander, and filthy language from your lips. Do not lie to each other, since you have taken off your old self with its practices and have put on the new self, which is being renewed in knowledge in the image of its Creator. Here there is no Greek or Jew, circumcised or uncircumcised, barbarian, Scythian, slave or free, but Christ is all, and is in all.*

*Therefore, as God's chosen people, holy and dearly loved, clothe yourselves with compassion, kindness, humility, gentleness and patience. Bear with each other and forgive whatever grievances you may have against one another. Forgive as the Lord forgave you. And over all these virtues put on love, which binds them all together in perfect unity* (Colossians 3:1-14 NIV).

DON'T expect your life to become completely sanctified immediately. But DO expect it to happen over time! Living a holy life is God's will for His children. Do you want to be living in the will of your Father? I know I do! The Holy Spirit will help you. In fact, it would be impossible to attain holiness without the help of the Holy Spirit. But you must also do your part!

Remember, God gave us a free will. It is up to us to conquer the lust of the eye, the lust of the flesh, and the pride of life! Begin by not allowing yourself to be in situations where you need to overcome temptation. Get rid of cable movie channels. Don't bring home R-rated movies from the video store. Don't open the first page of a trashy novel. Don't accept invitations to bars or parties that you know may be wild. As you move away from these kinds of activities, your sensitivity to sin will be heightened.

Ask the Lord to reveal to you areas of your life where you are not living within His will. Ask Him to show you the sin in your life, and then do your best to change those behaviors. As you consistently spend time reading and meditating on God's Word, He will reveal to you areas in which you need to grow.

Second Timothy 3:16-17 says, *All Scripture is given by inspiration of God, and is profitable for doctrine, for reproof, for correction, for instruction in righteousness, that the man of God may be complete, thoroughly equipped for every good work.* If you have a spouse or a close friend walking with the Lord, ask them to correct you, to help you to see areas in your life where you are not walking in love.

But most important, never lose sight of the blood that Jesus shed for you on the cross, opening the door to forgiveness for sin. When you miss it, go to Him immediately and repent. Repentance requires two actions from you. First, you must express a true, heartfelt sorrow for the sin you committed. And second, you must make an effort to turn away from that sin, to change, to grow in your walk by overcoming the temptation to repeat that sin again. But if you continue to miss it, go to your Father again and again and again and ask for forgiveness. First John 1:9 says, *If we confess our sins, He is faithful and just to forgive us our sins and to cleanse us from all unrighteousness.* Not only does our heavenly Father forgive us our sins, He also forgets them! *As far as the east is from the west, so far has He removed our transgressions from us* (Psalm 103:12). Hallelujah!

It is also important that you forgive yourself. Don't listen to Satan's lies saddling you with guilt for sins you've already repented for. Christ paid the price for your sin. You have been freed from all guilt! Instead, use situations where you've struggled to overcome sin as a springboard for renewal, for spiritual growth, and for service and ministry to others!

Therefore, strive for a life of holiness, walking in love, free from sin. When you do sin, repent and receive your forgiveness. And you will walk in the will of God every day of your long life!

## Chapter Twenty-six

# FORGIVENESS

*B*ack to those two tough questions: Why are some people healed, but not others, and why do bad things happen to good people? Another factor that can stand in the way of God's perfect will to heal is unforgiveness.

Mark 11:22-26 says: *So Jesus answered and said to them, "Have faith in God. For assuredly, I say to you, whoever says to this mountain, 'Be thou removed, and be cast into the sea,' and does not doubt in his heart, but believes that those things he says will be done, he will have whatever he says. Therefore I say to you, whatever things you ask when you pray, believe that you receive them, and you will have them. And whenever you stand praying, if you have anything against anyone, forgive him, that your Father in heaven may also forgive you your trespasses. But if you do not forgive, neither will your Father in heaven forgive your trespasses.*

In the last chapter, you read about the importance of being IN the perfect will of God, through sanctification and through confessing and repenting of all sin! However, if you have unforgiveness toward others in your heart, the Father will not forgive you of your sins. Thus you will <u>not</u> be in the perfect will of God, and you will <u>not</u> be able to receive the healing Jesus died to provide you with!

Let's look at more evidence in God's Word to support the importance of unconditional forgiveness.

✝ *Judge not, and you shall not be judged. Condemn not, and you shall not be condemned. Forgive, and you will be forgiven* (Luke 6:37).

✝ *"For if you forgive men their trespasses, your heavenly Father will also forgive you. But if you do not forgive men their trespasses, neither will your Father forgive your trespasses"* (Matthew 6:14-15).

✝ *Take heed to yourselves. If your brother sins against you, rebuke him; and if he repents, forgive him. And if he sins against you seven times in a day, and seven times in a day returns to you, saying, "I repent," you shall forgive him* (Luke 17:3-4).

✝ *And be kind to one another, tenderhearted, forgiving one another, even as God in Christ forgave you* (Ephesians 4:32).

The Word teaches that forgiveness is absolutely essential. But how do we forgive? How do we let go of the hurt, the offense, and the anger that fostered the unforgiveness in the first place? How do we break down long-standing walls of bitterness or rigid hard-heartedness that may have been built and fortified over many years?

Praise God, we have help! *I can do all things through Christ who strengthens me* (Philippians 4:13).

First of all, search your heart for any unforgiveness, resentment, or bitterness you may be harboring towards others. Take time to listen to the Holy Spirit within you, and He will reveal to you these areas. That's what He did for me. I was drawn to read Mark 11:22-26 over and over again. When you have a scripture that really speaks to you, I encourage you to take time to meditate on it. God has a special message or a revelation for you within His Word. When you meditate on scripture read it quietly and repeatedly. Talk to yourself as you think about it. Reflect on God's words spoken to you and His ways. Consider how to apply His message in your life.

As I meditated on Mark 11:22-26, I was focusing on the first part of the scripture which deals with believing without doubt, and God's promise that in doing so, we will receive what we are believing for. But that next part about forgiveness kept nagging at my spirit. As I meditated on it, I realized that in order for the prayer of faith to be effective, I absolutely had to release all unforgiveness and bitterness from my life.

As I examined my heart, I really didn't feel that I had any blatant unforgiveness residing there. But the Lord showed me that I had allowed seeds of offense to sprout into a root of bitterness in my heart towards my sister. With each small offense I had taken towards her in regards to our differences in parenting, a fence was erected, post by post and plank by plank. (Offence = of + fence.) Over the years, the fence caused division in my relationship with my sister and in my relationship with God! Offense is one of Satan's oldest tricks ... and I unknowingly fell for it!

Once you are aware of an area in your life in which you've allowed unforgiveness, bitterness, or offense to dwell, you must rid yourself of it. First, confess your unforgiveness to God and ask for His forgiveness of this sin.

But there's more. Repentance means a sincere desire to change, to turn away from your sin, and to make amends if at all possible with those whom you have sinned against. This sounds incredibly difficult. It is indeed very humbling to go before someone with whom you have a broken relationship and express your desire to repair it. But when you take the first baby step, the Holy Spirit will be right there beside you to give you the strength and the words to make things right.

Focus on reconciliation rather than resolution. Reconciliation centers around the relationship, while resolution centers around the problem. But when you focus on repairing the relationship, the problem often loses its significance.[2] I listened to the guidance of the Holy Spirit, and I went to work to repair the broken relationship with my sister.

Now, the other person may accept your forgiveness and/or apology and they may not. But you have done your part, and have repaired the chasm between yourself and your heavenly Father's forgiveness. The Lord calls us to forgive the offense. But He is the One to heal the wound in your heart. Healing starts in the spiritual realm and moves into the physical realm. You may still feel resentment or guilt regarding the bitterness or unforgiveness in your heart. But don't go by feelings. Remember 1 John 1:9: *If we confess our sins, He is faithful and*

---

[2]Rick Warren, *The Purpose Driven Life* (Grand Rapids, MI: Zondervan, 2002), 158.

*just to forgive us our sins and to cleanse us from all unrighteousness.*
You have been forgiven! Believe and receive God's grace!

Forgiveness does not mean that the other person did nothing wrong. For example, in the case of a woman who forgives her husband of physical abuse, the man is not released from his sin. Only his own heartfelt sorrow, confession, and repentance can do that. It is often the case that when we don't forgive, it's because we are hurt, and we feel the other person deserves to be hurt through our unforgiveness. However, harboring unforgiveness does <u>not</u> hurt the other person. Rather, it hurts <u>you</u>, because it stands in the way of you receiving God's forgiveness and healing – spiritual, emotional, or physical.

So forgive, and let God's healing begin!

## Chapter Twenty-seven

# SPIRITUAL WARFARE

You've already learned that it is not God's will for people to be sick. His perfect will is for divine health and healing. Satan is the author of sickness and disease. But in order for Satan to steal your health, he must have an open door.

The last six chapters have dealt with slamming the door shut in Satan's face! If you have surrendered your life and your heart to Jesus; if you have been baptized by the Holy Spirit; if you are developing your relationship with your Father through daily prayer, study of His Word, and praise and worship; if you are praying the prayer of faith and believing without doubt that you are healed in the name of Jesus and are confessing healing scriptures consistently; if you are in the will of God by obeying and living His Word, and confessing and repenting of any and all sin immediately; and if you are free from unforgiveness and bitterness ... **Satan cannot touch you!**

But he can sure try to get you to weaken and to fall back into your old ways! He will attack your thoughts first. The mind is the battlefield! In my case, after my all-clear surgeries, he pelted me with thoughts that the surgeries did not confirm that I was free of cancer in the lymph nodes in my neck (Chapter 15, "The Battle Continues"). As I allowed these thoughts to fester, Satan put symptoms in my body. And I believe that if I hadn't gone to war against Satan, he would have been successful to put cancer right there in the lymph nodes in my neck!

Remember, the believer has authority over Satan! *[The Father] has delivered and drawn us to Himself out of the control and the dominion of darkness...* (Colossians 1:13 AMP). *Behold, I give you the authority to trample on serpents and scorpions, and over all the power of the enemy, and nothing shall by any means hurt you* (Luke 10:19). But it is up to us to exercise that authority!

Not only did God deliver us from the control and dominion of darkness and give us authority over the enemy, He also provided us with mighty weapons for warfare! Ephesians 6:10-18 teaches us about our arsenal of weapons with which to battle the enemy. This scripture from Ephesians describes the full armor of God. Nothing is lacking. God provides all that we need to protect us defensively from Satan's attacks, and so that we can offensively keep him far away from our life! I've included the actual scripture in italics, and an explanation of the spiritual truth that each part of the armor symbolizes in parentheses.

*Finally, be strong in the Lord and in his mighty power. Put on the full armor of God so that you can take your stand against the devil's schemes. For our struggle is not against flesh and blood* (sickness or disease), *but against the rulers, against the authorities, against the powers of this dark world and against the spiritual forces of evil in the heavenly realms. Therefore put on the full armor of*

*God, so that when the day of evil comes, you may be able to stand your ground, and after you have done everything, to stand. Stand firm then, with the belt of truth buckled around your waist* (the belt of truth represents a <u>clear understanding of the Word of God</u>), *with the breastplate of righteousness in place* (the breastplate of righteousness means that <u>Jesus IS our righteousness</u>, and also represents <u>our obedience to the Word of God</u>; staying right with God), *and with your feet fitted with the readiness that comes from the gospel of peace* (the gospel of peace is <u>proclaiming</u> or <u>confessing</u> the Word of God). *In addition to all this, take up the shield of faith, with which you can extinguish all the flaming arrows of the evil one.* (the shield of faith represents our <u>complete safety under the blood of Christ</u>).

*Take the helmet of salvation,* (the helmet of salvation <u>protects our mind from doubt, or turning away from the truth</u>), *and the sword of the Spirit, which is the Word of God,* (the sword of the Spirit is <u>the Word of God used offensively as an active weapon against evil</u>). *And pray in the Spirit on all occasions and with all kinds of prayers and requests.* (To pray in the Spirit means to <u>pray in tongues as well as in your understanding</u>, <u>bringing your requests before God</u>.) (Ephesians 6:10-18 NIV).

Notice that almost the entire armor of God revolves around His Word. We are to study and understand the Word (which the Holy Spirit enables us to do). We are to obey the Word, proclaim (or confess) the Word, not turn away from the Word, and use the Word offensively as an active weapon against evil!

Even Jesus used the Word in spiritual warfare! Jesus Himself did not stand on His own strength as He was tempted by Satan, but on the strength of the Word of God! Right after Jesus was baptized and filled with the Holy Spirit, He *returned from the Jordan and was led by the Spirit into the wilderness, being tempted for forty days by the devil. And in those days He ate nothing, and afterward, when they had ended, He was hungry.*

*And the devil said to Him, "If you are the Son of God, command this stone to become bread."*

*But Jesus answered him, saying, "**It is written**, 'Man shall not live by bread alone, but by every word of God.'"*

*Then the devil, taking Him up on a high mountain, showed Him all the kingdoms of the world in a moment of time. And the devil said to Him, "All this authority I will give You, and their glory; for this has been delivered to me, and I give it to whomever I wish. Therefore, if You will worship before me, all will be Yours."*

*And Jesus answered and said to him, "Get behind Me, Satan! **For it is written**, 'You shall worship the Lord your God, and Him only you shall serve.'"*

*Then he brought Him to Jerusalem, set Him on the pinnacle of the temple, and said to Him, "If You are the Son of God, throw Yourself down from here. For it is written: 'He shall give His angels charge over you, to keep you,' and, 'In their hands they shall bear you up, lest you dash your foot against a stone.'"*

*And Jesus answered and said to him, "**It has been said**, 'You shall not tempt the Lord your God.'"*

*Now when the devil had ended every temptation, he departed from Him until an opportune time* (Luke 4:1-13).

---

But that was Jesus, the Son of God! How do <u>we</u> go about waging spiritual warfare against the enemy? We follow the teaching of God's Word! Let's go back and take a closer look at what the Word teaches us about the armor of God in Ephesians 6 NIV.

*Stand firm then, with the belt of truth buckled around your waist* … (v. 14). In order to use God's Word as your weapon, <u>you need it in you</u>! Once again, I stress the importance of daily devotions, time spent reading and studying the Word. Before you were saved, you were blinded to the Word, but now you see it with clarity! Each day that you read the Word, the Holy Spirit reveals new truths and understandings from God's Word to your mind and your spirit.

*With the breastplate of righteousness in place* … (v. 14). As we've already discussed in the Chapter 25, "Sanctification," we are also to <u>obey the Word</u>, to live according to its teaching! Through the grace of God, we are the righteousness of Christ Jesus, but in order to remain in God's right standing, we must live according to the Word! The epistles, the letters written by the apostles to the churches, are rich in teaching us how to live a holy, sanctified life. Unconfessed sin opens the door to Satan. Living a holy life, consecrated to the Lord, slams the door shut in Satan's face!

*And with your feet fitted with the readiness that comes from the gospel of peace* … (v. 15). We are to <u>proclaim God's Word</u>, first to ourselves, and then to the world. As we confess the Word over situations and circumstances in our lives, our faith muscles are strengthened and our ability to receive from God is opened to us. It is also our responsibility to take what we know and share it with others! Our commission is to save souls and to make disciples!

*And the sword of the Spirit, which is the word of God ...* (v. 17). <u>Use the Word</u> as an offensive weapon against Satan. As you confess healing scriptures over your body, you are negating Satan's lies of sickness and disease and professing God's truth of healing and abundant life! *For the law of the Spirit of life in Christ Jesus has made me free from the law of sin and death!* (Romans 8:2). Decide to choose life!

If Satan has attacked your body with sickness, confess the truth of God's healing over your body. But be prepared, because as you kick Satan out of your life, he's going to fight back with doubts, symptoms, or other circumstances. (Remember my lunch after the PET scan that came to exactly $6.66?) Here are some destructive bullets to shoot at Satan when he comes on the counterattack! (These scriptures have been personalized to use as confessions for spiritual warfare.)

- ✝ No weapon that the enemy sets up against me will prosper today, because God is my defense! (Isaiah 54:17).

- ✝ I am submitted to God, and the devil flees from me because I resist him in the name of Jesus! (James 4:7).

- ✝ I have authority over all the power of the enemy, and I destroy all of his works in Jesus' name! (Luke 10:19; 1 John 3:8).

*And pray in the Spirit on all occasions with all kinds of prayers and requests ...* (v. 18). Pray! Pray in the Spirit daily. Let me share an incredible testimony regarding the power of praying in tongues in defense against Satan. This happened one year after my all-clear from cancer.

I had had a follow-up CT scan to look for possible metastasis of cancer in my body. Two weeks after the CT scan, I had an appointment to go over the results with the oncologist. My husband was with me, and we had an extremely long wait in the waiting area (probably thanks to the enemy). Satan was having a heyday, filling my mind with worry and fear (false evidence appearing real). I knew better than voicing my fear, and I was trying to fight it with the Word. I read healing scriptures, but the fear didn't subside.

When we were called back into an examination room to wait again for the doctor, I asked my husband to pray for me. I was literally too consumed with fear to even form a prayer for myself. My husband prayed for me, but I still had this ridiculous fear. Then I began to pray in tongues. The <u>instant</u> the heavenly language came forth from my mouth, that lousy fear washed totally and completely away! It was physically tangible, the difference between the fear that was attacking me, and the faith and the peace that replaced it!

Praying in tongues is the perfect prayer, praying the perfect will of God, praying directly from the level of our spirit to God, without the mind getting in the way! Hallelujah!

We should also pray in the understanding. The Word tells us to bring our requests to God, to cast our cares upon Him, to trust Him, and He will give us the desires of our heart. He will give us peace, and He will answer our prayers! God is faithful to His Word, as long as we are doing our part and not standing in the way of His work!

*Put on the full armor of God, so that when the day of evil comes, you may be able to stand your ground, and after you have done everything, to stand* (v. 13). Stand on the Word! Don't give up! The situation you are walking through may not look like it's improving, but God's Word is always true and God's way is always perfect.

Remember, healing starts in the spiritual realm, and then moves into the physical realm. Our God is never too early or too late. He is always right on time. Be patient, be strong, and believe without doubting that you <u>are</u> the healed of the Lord!

## Chapter Twenty-eight

# GIVE GOD ALL THE GLORY!

*W*e are drawing to the close of this book, but not to the end of the blessed journey. This journey, the magnificent journey into the glory of God, is an eternal journey!

Let's review one last time. The journey of faith results in an abundant life ... today and all the days of your life, now and throughout eternity! These steps of the journey are not only important, they are <u>absolute vital necessities</u>. Follow God's plan, as outlined in His Word, and your life will be blessed with abundance, complete with healing and divine health. You will live each day in the glory of our mighty God!

- ✟ Surrender your life to Jesus. Accept Him as your Savior and the Lord of your life! With this surrender comes righteousness with God through His grace! With your salvation comes freedom from the grips of sin, sickness, and eternal death!
- ✟ Ask and receive the priceless gift of the baptism of the Holy Spirit, with the Bible evidence of speaking in tongues. With this gift comes the power to witness and to share the Good News with others!

- ✟ Develop a relationship with your Father – read and study the Word, fellowship with Him through prayer, and give Him your love through sincere praise and worship.
- ✟ Believe that you receive what you pray for. Remember that healing IS the will of God, as expressed in the truth of His Word. Confess the promises of God which are in His Word, over the circumstances in your life. Have faith!
- ✟ Obey the Word. Do the Word. Seek to grow in sanctification throughout every day of your life, developing your godly character. *But as the One Who called you is holy, you yourselves also be holy in all your conduct and manner of living. For it is written, You shall be holy, for I am holy* (1 Peter 1:15-16 AMP).
- ✟ Forgive everyone. Refuse the poison of bitterness in your life. It will inhibit God's forgiveness and blessings in your life.
- ✟ Fight back against the enemy! Exercise the authority Jesus provided for you as a believer when He died and rose again. *And having disarmed the powers and authorities, he made a public spectacle of them, triumphing over them by the cross!* (Colossians 2:15 NIV).

And that brings us to the final chapter in our blessed journey...

## Give God all the glory!

Mighty God, I pour out my heart and my love to You and give unto You all praise, all glory, and all honor. It's all about

You. It's not about me or about anything that I've done or earned. It's about Your grace, Your unmerited favor, Your gift to me of abundant life, of righteousness and justification in You. I give You the glory for my salvation, for my healing, for every breath that I breathe and every word that I speak. It's all about You, Lord, it's all about You!

I encourage you to share your testimonies of how God is working in your life, no matter how great or small, and give God all the glory! Testimonies bring hope to the hopeless. They provide direction to the lost. They energize faith! Testimonies draw souls to God. Do you realize that when you bring souls to God, you are giving God a gift, a treasure more precious than we can even comprehend?

God desires the fellowship of His children. That is the purpose for which we were created! The people that we lead to the Lord bring Him riches beyond compare, riches that He treasures more than anything. So share your testimonies! Be bold! Ephesians 6:19-20 AMP is a prayer that you can pray for this very purpose: I pray *that [freedom of] utterance may be given me, that I may open my mouth to proclaim boldly the mystery of the good news (the Gospel), for which I am an ambassador ... I [ pray] that I may declare it boldly and courageously, as I ought to do.*

Keep a prayer journal and document all of your prayers and their answers! (My prayer journal was the foundation for this book!) Then share your answered prayers, your "God incidences" with everyone! Be a big mouth for God! Allow Him to lead you, to use you. But be prepared, because when you tell

God that you desire to serve Him, He <u>will</u> open doors, and you may not be so sure you are ready or that you can handle what He's asking of you. Be assured that you can, because you have the anointing of the Holy Spirit and the power of prayer!

That's why and how I wrote this book. God wants me to share my testimony, and He has prepared the way for me to do so. First, He led me to minister to others diagnosed with cancer, sharing both my testimony and His Word about healing. Then He led me to go to another level, to write this book. In this format, the testimony God gave me will spread further, and possibly with more clarity than with only the spoken Word.

I am in awe of the privilege God has provided me to share my testimony with so many cancer patients. And I am in awe of the healings that I have seen over and over and over again, when His children simply believe with all their hearts and strive to do His will in their lives. Praise God, He doesn't seek perfection; rather, He sees your heart and your love for Him.

This book is for my God and for His people. His great commandment says, *"Love the Lord your God with all your heart and with all your soul and with all your mind." This is the first and greatest commandment. And the second is like it: "Love your neighbor as yourself"* (Matthew 22:37-39 NIV). I do love God with all of my being, and He is first priority in my life. He is magnificent, greater than cancer, greater than any obstacle Satan may throw into my life. I give Him the glory for my healing, and for the healing of Karie, Tom, Brendan, Gary, and Ben, along with many others whom I've had the honor of ministering to and praying with. And now I have spread my testimony to you, believing with an unwavering faith, that you too, are the healed of the Lord!

*I shall not die, but live, and declare the works of the Lord.*
Psalm 118:17

Every morning when I open my eyes, I rejoice in a new day. I embrace each day as a priceless gift from God! Every day, every minute, every breath of life truly is a precious gift from God. God gave my life to me, and now I offer it back to Him. I spread my testimony throughout the world. I dedicate my life to serving my God and His people! And I give God all of the glory!

*For now and forever,
my journey continues ...*